TWENTIETH
CENTURY
WORLD
HISTORY

LATIN AMERICA

IN THE TWENTIETH CENTURY

JOHN GRIFFITHS

Batsford Academic and Educational   *London*

CONTENTS

ACKNOWLEDGMENT

The Author and Publishers thank the following for their kind permission to reproduce copyright illustrations: Camera Press Ltd for figs 1, 2, 3, 4, 5, 7, 8, 9, 10, 11, 16, 18, 19, 20, 21, 22, 26, 27, 28, 31, 32, 33, 39, 46, 50, 52, 57, 58; Popperfoto for figs 29, 34, 35, 48, 51, 54; Topham Picture Library for figs 14, 15, 17, 24, 25, 30, 36, 37, 44, 45. Figs 6, 38, 40, 43, 49, 56 and 59 were reprinted from *Latin America in Caricature* by John J. Johnson (University of Texas Press, Austin and London) (Tony Auth, fig 38; Herblock Cartoons, figs 6, 43; Los Angeles Times Syndicate, fig 49; Bill Mauldin, fig 59; Richard Q. Yardley, figs 40, 56). Figs 42 and 47 are copyright of the Author. Figs 12 and 13 were drawn by R.F. Brien. Special thanks to Lucy Chamberlain for typing the manuscript.

© John Griffiths 1985
First published 1985

Typeset by Tek-Art Ltd, Kent
and printed in Great Britain by
R.J. Acford
Chichester, Sussex
for the publishers
Batsford Academic and Educational,
an imprint of B. T. Batsford Ltd,
4 Fitzhardinge Street
London W1H 0AH

ISBN 0 7134 3840 1

THE GEOGRAPHICAL PERSPECTIVE

It is people who make history but not always in the fashion they would necessarily choose. They are constrained by numerous factors, not least the legacy of past people's contribution to history. These people, in their turn, have been restricted by the geography of the area they have inhabited. The geographical characteristics of Latin America, as we shall see, continue to exert a force on the present just as they have in the past.

FROM RIO GRANDE TO TIERRA DEL FUEGO

Latin America is an enormous area to comprehend. It stretches from the Rio Grande, cutting off North from South America, to Tierra del Fuego at the southernmost tip of South America. From North America, Latin America stretches through Central America to the continent of South America, as well as taking in some outposts in the Caribbean – an area which is increasingly caught up in the events in, and influences of, mainland Latin America. The area covered amounts to some eight million square miles, representing about fifteen per cent of the earth's land area.

Not surprisingly, the countries in such a vast area show great disparities in size, resources and development. Brazil, for example, is the fifth largest country in the world, possessing vast resources which are only beginning to be exploited. Brazil has reached a level of development that has been described as an "economic miracle". Even so, within Brazil there is still great inequality, poverty and deprivation, some of it caused by the "economic miracle" itself. Mexico and Argentina are, similarly, gigantic countries, both of which have shown dramatic social and economic developments in the twentieth century. At the other end of the scale, El Salvador, in Central America, is a country the size of Wales, with little in the way of resources. Cuba, in the Caribbean, a country the size of England, has enormous agricultural and industrial potential.

1 A huge statue of Christ looms over Rio de Janeiro in Brazil. The city has grown phenomenally in the twentieth century.

2 The Andes mountains look down on La Paz, the capital of Bolivia. Like all Latin American cities, La Paz is a mixture of ostentatious wealth and miserable poverty. In the rainy season the adobe houses, made of hard-packed earth, on the highest slopes of the mountain slide down towards the more prosperous areas.

Most of Latin America falls within the tropics but it is far from being a tropical area; a great deal of economic activity, for geographical reasons, has taken place in mountainous regions.

When Hernan Cortes was asked to describe Mexico he is said to have crumpled a piece of paper in his hand to show the essentially mountainous nature of the country. Central America is also mountainous, with most settlement having occurred well above sea level, and lowland area, as in Mexico, a rarity. The Panama Canal, cutting across Central America, is only possible because of a gap in two mountain ranges.

Central America is of the same geographical structure as the Greater Antilles – Cuba, the Dominican Republic and Haiti are made up of the same mountain systems as their Central American neighbours, Guatemala, Honduras and Nicaragua. Hispaniola (Haiti and the Dominican Republic) is extremely mountainous whilst Cuba is predominantly gently undulating agricultural land.

3 The snow-capped Andes mountains contrast with the plateau region of Bolivia.

South America represents seven eighths of Latin America's surface area. Down the western side of the continent run the Andes Mountains which take up a quarter of its area, cutting off the east from the west and towering majestically above all its activities. The Andes run for over four thousand miles, from Tierra del Fuego to Chile where the mountains divide into two in Northern Argentina, Bolivia and Peru. In Bolivia the Andes are four hundred miles wide and near La Paz, Bolivia's capital, rise to twenty thousand feet. In Peru the two mountain ranges converge only to split into three. One part vanishes into the Amazon, the other two splitting and converging through Ecuador, Colombia and Venezuela with the last trace of the Andes on the island of Trinidad. Of relatively recent origin, the Andes are still geographically active and capable of eruption, as occurred in the Peruvian Andes in 1970 when 50,000 people lost their lives.

4   The Amazonian rain forests of Brazil represent not only a vast, barely-tapped resource for the country but also, perhaps, survival for the rest of the world. The exploitation of this region in recent times has raised concerns about the possible harmful effects on the Earth's atmosphere.

On the eastern slopes of the Andes there are highly fertile, inhabitable areas, like the *yungas* of Bolivia, which run into the lowland region. The western slopes are steep and inhospitable. The eastern highlands of South America are made up of the Brazilian plateau, covering a million square miles (by far the most important area), the Guiana Massif mountain range in Venezuela and Brazil and the Patagonian plateau in the south of Argentina.

In the lowland region of South America it is the Amazon which grasps our attention. This is the largest river in the world, at some 4,500 miles.

With all its tributaries, it represents twenty thousand miles of navigable waterways, and is doubled in times of flooding.

The Amazon is connected to the Orinoco river, the basin of which consists of the *llanos* of Colombia and Venezuela where cattle and horses are raised in inhospitable conditions.

By contrast, the Amazonian lowlands are the largest area of forest land in the world and of considerable importance to the earth's ecology. Recent destruction of the Amazonian rain forests represents a threat to the earth's ecological balance.

The southernmost lowland area of South America is the Argentine *pampa*, covering a quarter of a million miles. This area is rich, fertile and temperate, in contrast to much of the continent.

POPULATION

The indigenous Indians of what was to become Latin America were devastated by diseases like measles, influenza and smallpox brought from Europe by the Spanish. The Inca empire that stretched across the Andes may have contained as many as twelve million people at the time of the Spanish Conquest. By the 1570s this had fallen to one and a half million. Elsewhere in Latin America Indian peoples died off and entire tribes disappeared.

that now characterizes Latin America. The Europeans were producing children of mixed descent, the *mestizos*, through inter-marriage with Indians. *Mestizos* occupied, and still occupy, a middle position in society, in which whites are the most wealthy and powerful. Black people were introduced as slaves from Africa, forming another ethnic group in Latin America. In their turn, they were to inter-mix with whites, *mestizos* and Indians, so adding to the racial diversity of the region.

By the eighteenth century Latin America's population was already growing, to be further stimulated in the nineteenth century by the world demand for Latin American mineral and agricultural products. New areas were settled and immigrants were attracted to the region. But it is

the twentieth century that has witnessed the most profound population explosion, which has often outstripped production.

The effects of immigration were confined to particular Latin American countries. Argentina, Uruguay and Brazil were particularly affected. From 1884-1954 Brazil accepted 4.5 million immigrants from Europe, mostly Portugal and Italy. From 1881-1935 3.5 million entered Argentina, and nearly three quarters of a million Uruguay. The famous *Golondrinas* ("swallows") from Italy as well as from Portugal were the largest group. Many returned home but a growing number remained. In other countries, like Venezuela, immigrants from other Latin American and Caribbean countries have increased populations.

5 In the midst of Mexico's "Economic Miracle" of the 1970s and '80s, this woman is forced to rummage in rubbish tips for her living.

Better health facilities, better diet and water supplies have reduced death rates, especially in urban areas and particularly after the 1940s. The death rate fell but the high birth rates increased. The result was a dramatic increase in numbers. The countries with the best economic development have experienced the highest rates of population growth, with the added phenomenon of the shift of people from countryside to towns and cities. Most population growth in Latin America since the 1950s has been in urban areas.

Brazil's population grew by 49 million from 1960-79, 43 million of that figure in cities or towns. Lima, in Peru, grew by one million from 1970-80. The Cuban Census of 1981 shows the shift from countryside to town: in 1970 60.5 per cent of the population were urban-dwellers; by 1981 this figure had risen to 69 per cent, with total population increasing by 1 million.

People migrate from the countryside to the towns because they think they will improve their lot. Most of those who do migrate are young, single or recently married and, therefore, more likely themselves to contribute to further population growth.

The expectations of those who go to the towns and cities are not always realized. Housing and employment, because of the growth of demand for them, have become scarce. The growth of industries has not kept pace with the growth of population so there are few jobs of that kind to be had. Rather, the newcomers to the cities must take low-paid, unskilled jobs. In the 1980s, when the effects of the world economic crisis were visible throughout Latin America, fewer of even these jobs were available. Increasingly, people resorted to selling on the streets, begging, scavenging and prostitution, simply to remain alive. For many

Latin America's Population Growth*

	1900 (unless otherwise stated)	1940 (unless otherwise stated)	1970 (unless otherwise stated)	1980
Argentina	3,954,911 (1895)	15,897,127 (1947)	23,364,431	27,720,000
Bolivia	1,696,400	3,019,031 (1950)	4,687,716 (1976)	5,600,000
Brazil	17,318,556	41,236,315	93,215,311	120,287,000
Chile	2,507,005 (1895)	5,023,539	8,836,223	11,104,000
Colombia	4,143,632 (1905)	8,701,816 (1938)	21,070,115 (1973)	26,115,000
Costa Rica	243,205 (1892)	800,875 (1950)	1,871,780 (1973)	2,223,000
Cuba	1,572,797 (1899)	4,778,583 (1943)	8,553,395	9,706,000
Dominican Republic	894,665 (1920)	2,135,872 (1950)	4,009,458	5,431,000
Ecuador	—	3,202,757 (1950)	6,500,845 (1974)	7,996,000
El Salvador	—	1,855,917 (1950)	3,549,260 (1971)	4,813,000
Guatemala	1,364,678 (1893)	2,222,000	5,211,929 (1973)	7,053,000
Haiti	1,631,260 (1918)	3,097,222 (1950)	4,314,628 (1971)	5,008,000
Honduras	331,917 (1881)	1,107,859	2,653,857 (1974)	3,691,000
Mexico	13,607,259	19,653,552	48,225,238	69,900,000
Nicaragua	505,377 (1906)	983,000	1,894,690 (1971)	2,422,000
Panama	336,742 (1911)	622,576	1,428,082	1,837,000
Paraguay	931,799 (1936)	1,328,452 (1950)	2,354,071 (1972)	3,168,000
Peru	2,651,840 (1876)	6,208,000	13,567,939 (1972)	17,624,000
Uruguay	1,042,686 (1908)	2,595,510 (1963)	2,763,964 (1975)	2,921,000
Venezuela	2,323,527 (1891)	3,850,771 (1941)	10,721,522	15,061,000

*A word of warning about population figures. They are at best always an approximation. Special care should always be taken with historical data.

The Other Latin-American Summit

6 In 1967 Latin America's leaders met at a "summit" meeting in Uruguay to discuss economic problems. Using the word "summit" literally, this cartoon points to the basic problems of inequality and misery suffered by most Latin American countries.

people, the move to the towns was not accompanied by the hoped-for bettering of their standard of living.

In sharp contrast to the urban poor are the well-off, concentrated in particular areas of the towns and cities. The growth of cities has led to greater inequalities in Latin America. The well-off are usually people who are involved in activities like those in the cities of the USA or Western Europe – commerce, banking and the like. They have no experience of the deprivation suffered by the poor with whom they would have only the most tenuous contact.

A poor woman living in a shanty-town outside Lima, or Saõ Paulo, or Caracas might work for a

pittance as a maid in the home of a middle-class or upper-class family. Her life and theirs could not be more different. For all shanty-town dwellers, no matter where the location, there is a shared poverty. Homes, if they can be called that, are flimsily made of cardboard or straw matting or any building material that can be found. All the makeshift buildings are in a poor area, perhaps by marshy ground or on the side of a mountain, with no sanitation and inadequate or no water supplies. Poor health, poverty and malnutrition characterize these places. Thousands of children die each year from the appalling conditions into which they are born. In some shanty-towns there is an optimism, that "things must get better"; in others, only despair.

YOUNG HISTORIAN

A
1 List ways in which geography has influenced history. What other factors besides geography influence history?
2 Make a "league table" of Latin American countries by (a) area and (b) population. Are there any marked differences?
3 Find out more about (a) the Andes and (b) the Amazon. Which other Latin American geographical features are noteworthy?
4 How does Latin America's population growth compare with (a) Africa's and (b) Europe's?
5 List all the reasons why people move to the towns and cities in Latin America.

B

Imagine you are Hernan Cortes; write a letter home describing the land (Mexico) you have "discovered".

C

You are a journalist visiting a shanty town in a Latin American city. What would you want to know about the lives of the people there?

D

On an outline map of Latin America draw in the most important mountains and rivers.

Some Facts about Latin America

	Area(km^2)	Projected population in 1990	Life Expectancy	% Urban in 1980	% Literacy	Economy
Argentina	2,776,656	32,356,000	69.4(1975/80)	85.7	93.7('80)	Agriculture
Bolivia	1,098,581	7,302,000	48.6(1975/80)	32.7	63.2('76)	Agriculture, mining, petrol/gas
Brazil	8,511,965	156,239,000	63.4(1975/80)	67.6	70.3('78)	Agriculture, manufacturing
Chile	756,629	13,160,000	65.7(1975/80)	81.5	94.0('79)	Agriculture, mining
Colombia	1,138,338	32,116,000	61.0(1980)	76.3	77.6('80)	Agriculture, manufacturing
Costa Rica	50,900	2,885,000	70.0(1978)	45.9	89.8('78)	Agriculture, man., commerce
Cuba	110,922	—	71.9(1980)	69.0	96.9('80)	Agriculture, man., mining
Dominican Republic	48,442	6,792,000	55.4(1970)	53.5	66.3('76)	Agriculture, mining, tourism
Ecuador	270,670	10,744,000	—	43.5	78.0('80)	Agriculture, industry, oil/gas
El Salvador	20,935	6,472,000	59.0(1980)	40.3	40.0('71)	Agriculture
Guatemala	108,889	9,459,000	57.8(1975/80)	32.3	45.4('73)	Agriculture
Haiti	27,750	5,928,000	52.7(1975/80)	25.0	23.0('78)	Agriculture, mining
Honduras	112,088	5,029,000	55.5(1980)	35.9	40.5('80)	Agriculture, fishing
Mexico	1,967,183	97,568,000	65.0(1980)	69.0	78.0('80)	Agriculture, man., oil/gas
Nicaragua	139,000	3,074,000	55.2(1975/80)	57.8	88.0('82)	Agriculture, manufacturing
Panama	77,082	2,254,000	69.1(1975)	53.8	79.3('70)	Services
Paraguay	406,752	4,029,000	65.1(1980)	36.5	80.5('80)	Agriculture, manufacturing
Peru	1,280,219	22,959,000	57.2(1975/80)	70.5	79.7('78)	Mining, agric., fishing, oil
Uruguay	186,926	3,086,000	72.0(1980)	81.3	89.8('80)	Agriculture, manufacturing
Venezuela	898,805	21,138,000	66.4(1975/80)	77.7	82.0('77)	Oil, agric., man., mining

THE LEGACY OF THE PAST

Fidel Castro has spoken of Cuba as an *Afro-Hispanic* society, stressing the contribution made to Cuba's development and culture by her African population. Haya de la Torre, drawing on the history of the Andean countries and of Mexico, emphasized the *Indian* legacy in Latin America. It is often said that Latin America is the result of the collision of two worlds, Europe and America. In fact, many worlds have collided, and continue to collide, with Latin America, adding to its cultural richness and diversity.

EARLY SETTLEMENT

Before European colonization native Indian people had lived for thousands of years in Latin America. Their agriculture was well-developed and they enjoyed a high standard of living. At the time of the Spanish Conquest American Indians certainly enjoyed a higher standard of living than their "conquerors". Indian staple foods, like potatoes, were to revolutionize the diets of other societies.

There were great civilizations. In Bolivia there was the impressive Tihuanacu society. Throughout the Andes the great Inca civilization has left its mark, in the sophisticated irrigation and terracing that supported its advanced agricultural system. In Mexico the architecture of the Aztecs continues to dazzle and amaze. Many of the urban centres of that time, located in favourable environments, were taken over by the

7 The ancient pre-Inca site of Tihuanacu, near Lake Titicaca on the Bolivian-Peruvian border, remains something of a mystery. It could have been a religious centre, a market, or the centre of a vast empire like that of the Incas who built upon the Tihuanacu civilization.

8 Before the much better-known Aztecs in Mexico, great cities like this one at El Tajin were constructed as part of the Toltec civilization.

"conquerors" and incorporated into their own Empires. Cuzco in Peru is an example; it became an important Spanish settlement and maintains its Inca architecture to the present.

The Indian populations were soon decimated by their contact with Europe. Whole tribes disappeared, although a visit to Peru, Bolivia or Mexico will show the existence of indigenous people. In the highlands of Bolivia and Peru the

11

people keep to a style of life which originated in Latin America before Columbus. Some of the small tribes still exist, like the Guarani in Paraguay and the Mapuchi Indians of Chile.

The conquest of the "New World", as the Spanish called Latin America, was to transform the region. New languages, Spanish and Portuguese, were introduced along with new cultures, new religions and new forms of organization and

9 Camajura Indians in Brazil are just one example of pre-Colombian societies still living in Latin America.

10 Markets, like this one in Antigua, Guatemala, have existed for centuries throughout Latin America, performing an important social as well as economic function.

12

the rest of the region. These centres have lasted as the provincial towns of today.

Since the Spanish were primarily interested in extracting the riches of the New World, it was necessary to establish an efficient system of ports to enable their transport to Europe. The locations of important mines, like the famous silver mine of Potosi in Bolivia, also determined where towns developed.

MINES AND PLANTATIONS

The Spanish took over the *mita* labour system of the Incas but with none of the support the Indians could have expected under the Incas. The Indians were worked to death in the extraction of gold and silver from the mines. In the first 150 years of the new Spanish Empire nearly 19,000 tons of silver and 200 tons of gold were officially shipped to Spain. It has been said that a bridge of silver could have stretched from the New World to Spain, matched by a similar bridge made from the bones of those who died in its extraction. The gold and silver mined paid for the costs of Empire and made rich the nobility of Spain and Portugal. But it could not last for ever. By 1600 there was a decline in the mines' production and new forms of economic activity had to be found. This was the age of the *hacienda* and the plantation.

The *hacienda* (*estancia* in Argentina, *fazenda* in Brazil) were developed as huge estates producing a variety of crops and raising cattle. The landowner, the *hacendado*, possessed not only wealth but great power. The *Casa Grande*, the big house of the *hacendado*, would dominate and control the area of the *hacienda*, the lands of which would be taken from the local Indians who were then forced to work on the estate. The *haciendas* of the sixteenth and seventeenth centuries have lasted to the present, bringing with them the racist and elitist values of that time.

The plantation system began in Brazil for the production of one crop, sugar-cane, for the export

administration. From the moment the first Spaniard set foot in the New World, the old world was doomed.

The Spanish and Portuguese settlements in the sixteenth century, sometimes on the sites of existing Indian centres, were the foundation of present-day towns and cities. The Spanish contact with Latin America was more profound than the Portuguese, for Portugal was more concerned with her colonies in Africa and Asia than with laying claim to new responsibilities. Brazil, therefore, had just a few Portuguese settlements along the coast, a pattern of development that existed to the twentieth century. The Spanish took over existing Indian centres from which to colonize and subject of sugar, molasses and rum to Europe. The system quickly spread to the production of other crops like cotton and tobacco. Plantations and slavery went hand in hand. More than ten million slaves made the crossing from Africa to the New World from the seventeenth century until the abolition of the slave trade in the nineteenth century. Brazil's and Cuba's development were especially dependent upon slavery, and the racial conflict experienced by both countries in the twentieth century was but one result.

The large landholdings were more than just economic units. They were, as was seen in the southern states of the US, a way of life. The *hacienda* had political power and the *hacendado* was of some local, sometimes national importance. It is from the large estates that the traditional Latin American *caudillo*, the strong, virile leader, was to emerge.

ENGLISH, FRENCH AND DUTCH INTERESTS

By the seventeenth century other European powers were questioning Spain's and Portugal's control of the New World. The buccaneering exploits of Sir Francis Drake and John Hawkins were but the prelude to greater English interest in the region since in 1655 the country had a foothold in Jamaica. The French took an interest in Brazil, but were unable to maintain a permanent settlement there. More successful were the Dutch, who were able to maintain a considerable part of Brazilian coastal territory in the North East.

The eighteenth century saw the extension of European wars to Latin America but without any lasting effect upon Spanish and Portuguese control. England did gain a lucrative entry to the Spanish slave and colonial trade that was to put her in good stead on the independence of Latin America.

STRUGGLES FOR INDEPENDENCE

For three hundred years the Spanish controlled the New World but by 1815 there was nothing in Spanish hands except Cuba and Puerto Rico. The independence struggles were no sudden phenomenon but the result of a long build-up of resentment by the *criollos* (creoles, whites born in Latin America), black slaves and Indian serfs and the *mestizos* (of white and Indian blood), as well as new immigrants.

Even before the end of the eighteenth century there were uprisings by oppressed slaves and Indians. The legendary Tupac Amaru with seventy thousand men controlled Peru, Bolivia and Northern Argentina. Slaves were constantly in revolt in Brazil and Cuba. In Brazil twenty thousand established their own free society before being destroyed by a massive military campaign. In Haiti the first black republic was set up, after driving out the British in 1798 and seeing off twenty-five thousand French. There was creole unrest too, stemming from opposition to the new economic laws imposed by the Spanish, an interest in the ideas of the Enlightenment, that in the hands of some were revolutionary weapons, and from resentment at the expulsion of Jesuits from Latin America at the end of the eighteenth century. Creoles particularly resented their exclusion from positions of power and responsibility which always went to *peninsulares* (whites from Spain). What emerged was a strong sense of "nationalism" even though, at this time, the Latin American nations had not been formed. Creoles began to assert their American-ness, insisting that they were not Spanish. The literature of the time, that extolled the beauty and richness of the region, confirmed their growing identification with America.

Spain attempted to increase her control of her colonies in the years close to independence. When in 1807 Napoleon marched into Spain and put his brother Joseph on the throne, it was the signal for Latin America to break free. The revolutions for independence broke across the entire area with a violence and suddenness that surprised the participants. Such was the extent of the feeling against Spain.

The results of the wars of independence could be said to be felt still throughout Latin America. The wars caused great destruction and chaos out of which it was necessary to build a new society, free from Spain. The need to bring order out of the

VICEROYALTY OF
NEW SPAIN

Vera
Cruz

CAPTAINCY-GENERAL
OF CUBA

CAPTAINCY-GENERAL
OF GUATEMALA

Porto Bello

Cartagena

VICEROYALTY OF NEW
GRANADA

Captaincy-Gen.
of Venezuela

GUIANAS

ATLANTIC

Presidency of
Quito

VICEROYALTY
OF PERU

VICEROYALTY   OF

BRAZIL

PACIFIC

OCEAN

Presidency of
Charcas

Paraguay

OCEAN

VICEROYALTY

OF

LA PLATA

Banda
Oriental

CAPTAINCY-GENERAL OF CHILE

0   1000

Kilometres

13 Latin America today. The dates shown are dates of independence.

chaos resulted in the rise of the political power of the military and this, in its turn, led to a tendency towards conservative policies.

The stability brought by the military was desirable, the closing-off of chances for social improvement much less so. Slaves and Indians involved in the struggle were to find their positions little improved by the freedom from Spain. Upper-class and creole fears of "another Haiti", where black slaves had set up their own free republic, ensured that blacks and Indians stood no chance of advancement. Nor was the anticipated rise of the creoles forthcoming. Little had changed, it would appear, other than having got rid of Spain.

BRITISH INVOLVEMENT IN LATIN AMERICA

The newly independent states saw their development linked to Britain. Britain was the most industrially developed country in the world. British loans and political support were seen as vital to the survival of the new nations. It was to London that the "liberators" went to seek support for their new regimes and where the Foreign Minister Canning was to remark: "I called a new world into existence to redress the balance of the old." It was a new economic world.

Contemporary Latin American accounts speak of the ostentatious wealth of the British traders and merchants who flocked to Latin America, drawn by its *El Dorado* reputation. Floods of ill-chosen goods, like ice-skates and warming pans, arrived at Latin American ports. The British were selling not buying. The result was nothing short of catastrophe for local producers and traders. British goods, like textiles, replaced locally made products. A new commercial system based on ready cash pushed out local traders dependent upon credit. New products, new fashions, new lifestyles were offered by the British, but at a price. The frenzy of consumption of Latin America's upper class drained the area of capital for development. The City of London obliged by providing funds, over £21 million between 1822 and 1825. The story is a shameful one. The Latin American countries which raised the loans

received less than half their nominal value and much of the money, anyway, was destined as debts owed to British merchant houses. Capital was not to flow in any volume from London to Latin America until much later in the nineteenth century.

INTEGRATION INTO THE WORLD ECONOMY

By the second half of the nineteenth century most Latin American countries had entered a more settled, peaceful period. This was a time when international trade was growing (between the 1820s and World War I it was to grow by twenty-seven times) and Latin America became caught up in the expansion. The economic relationships established at that time were to set the pattern for future developments. Latin America became the source of raw materials, minerals and agricultural products for Europe and, later, for North America – a relationship that has proved difficult to change. Argentina and Uruguay produced cereals and meat, mostly for the British market; Brazil, Colombia, Ecuador, Cuba and Central America produced sugar, coffee and tobacco; Chile, Peru, Bolivia and Mexico produced minerals; later, Venezuela and Mexico were to be important sources of oil.

Capital began to flow to Latin America again. On the eve of the First World War foreign capital in Latin America stood at £1,700 million. Most came from Britain, the rest from France, Germany and the US. One fifth of all British investments abroad were in Latin America, with Argentina taking the most part.

With the inflow of capital came immigrants with energy and optimism, and the latest technical innovations like railways, electric street lights and telephones. Agriculture and mining received up-to-date technical guidance from abroad, contributing to a phenomenal increase in production. The development of refrigerated shipping, *frigorificos*, from the 1880s enabled Argentine beef and mutton to be shipped to European tables.

Latin American landowners, like the *estancieros* of Argentina, became astronomically rich. Their political power grew with their wealth, little of which was directed into investments at home. Few at that time were aware of the dangers of monoculture or mono-production. In times of prosperity there was little thought that an alternative source of nitrates would be found, or demand for sugar or coffee depressed. Nor was the extent to which foreign interests controlled the most important resources questioned. After World War I, and even more so in the depressed conditions of the 1930s, the problems of foreign control and monoculture were to loom especially large.

YOUNG HISTORIAN

A

1 Find out more about the early inhabitants of Latin America.
2 Write a project on *either* the Aztecs *or* the Incas.
3 Make a list of all the reasons for the fight for Latin American independence. Who were the "Liberators"?
4 Was independence "good" for Latin America?
5 What benefits went to Latin America from being caught up in world trade at the end of the nineteenth century?
6 Find examples of monoculture in areas other than Latin America.

B

Imagine you are on a ship bringing the first shipment of beef from Argentina to Britain in the 1880s. Write about what it was like leaving Buenos Aires and then arriving at London Docks.

C

Show on a map where the different European countries left their mark on Latin America.

D

Use some Inca or Aztec patterns in a design of your own.

DEVELOPMENT AND DEPRESSION

Latin American developments in the late nineteenth century, based upon increasing exports of agricultural and mineral products, were not radically different from the Iberian (Spanish and Portuguese) colonial pattern. What was new was the involvement of other European powers who were able massively to develop the exports of raw materials and goods necessary to their own industrial development. Although slavery had been abolished (not until the 1880s in the case of Cuba and Brazil), other forms of forced labour took its place and even grew in response to external demands. The colonial relationship persisted – some would say increased – during this period, with Latin American exports to countries like Britain simply organized in a more efficient manner.

14 *Gauchos* **on Argentina's vast cattle ranges in the** *Pampas* **carry on a way of living and working that has existed for hundreds of years. Just a few** *Gauchos* **and their dogs can control hundreds of cattle.**

A CASE STUDY: BRAZIL

15 1940s. Selecting meat for the production of corned beef; a semi-skilled job that was one of the few job opportunities for women in Argentina.

Brazil exemplifies the boom–slump, cyclical nature of Latin America's economic links with the rest of the world. The first cycle was based upon red dyewood, the *Pau brasil* which gave Brazil its name. Then, by the end of the sixteenth century, sugar was the main plank of Brazil's economy and the country was soon to be competing with the Caribbean sugar-producers. Cotton and other crops were grown in a vain attempt to avoid alternating booms and slumps. Gold discoveries in the eighteenth century provided further short-lived prosperity.

The taste for coffee in Europe and North America in the early nineteenth century caused another boom and Brazil was able to maintain a monopoly over coffee production until the twentieth century when other Latin American countries like Colombia, El Salvador and Nicaragua entered the scene as coffee-producers.

At the end of the nineteenth century rubber had a short-lived boom, until production in Asia, from seeds smuggled out of Brazil, destroyed Brazil's monopoly. Coffee remained as the main sector of the Brazilian economy (by 1951 accounting for over 60 per cent of exports).

By the 1920s São Paulo alone could produce all the coffee the world demanded. Over-production in Brazil and other countries caused violent fluctuations in the price; the familiar boom and slump experience. What could be done? States producing coffee attempted to control prices by buying up stocks to release onto the market when prices were high. This system worked until the 1930s when the world depression cut the ground from beneath all producers of agricultural goods, making a re-evaluation of economic policies all the more necessary.

Brazil's cycles of boom and slump were repeated

21

elsewhere in Latin America. Peru enjoyed a short-lived prosperity from its exports of *guano* (fertilizer) which were replaced on the world market by nitrates from Chile to be replaced, in their turn, during the First World War, by synthetic nitrates. Cuba, dependent throughout the twentieth century on a single product, sugar, was at the mercy of the ups and downs of world demand. In times of depression, as in the 1930s, widespread suffering resulted. Bolivia's dependence on tin exports provides a similar picture.

INDUSTRIALIZATION

The late nineteenth/early twentieth-century exports of raw materials from Latin America were to benefit industries in other parts of the world. What was stopping Latin American countries using these resources themselves, for their own industrialization and development? Latin American countries were poorly placed to industrialize in the early twentieth century; education levels were low, roads and railways and other means of communication were generally poor. Skills and capital to get industries moving have been scarce. Even so, Latin America has begun to industrialize and countries like Brazil, Argentina and Mexico are in the forefront of this development.

Spain and Portugal actively discouraged the development of industries and, although there were some local industries and artisans, larger-scale manufacturing did not appear until the end of the nineteenth century and even then was geared up to the burgeoning export industries. In Argentina and Uruguay the export of meat required large-scale slaughter-houses, freezing

16 These Bolivian tin-miners look remarkably happy, given the miserable life they must endure. Tin-miners rarely live past the age of thirty, working in the dangerous and unhealthy conditions of the mines.

17 The open-cast copper mine at Chuquicamata in Chile, the largest of its kind in the world.

plants, canning factories for the production of "corned" beef, factories for meat extracts and leather plants. An infrastructure based upon exports developed. The railways came to Latin America but only to enable goods to be carried to the coast for export and, because of high transport costs, manufacturing tended to congregate near to the ports – hence, the rise of port-cities, like Buenos Aires, which stimulated the growth of small industries based upon food, drink and clothing. Much of this early manufacturing was dependent upon skills and capital from abroad.

After the First World War, and especially during the world depression of the 1930s, demand for Latin American agricultural and mineral products was dramatically reduced. As Latin America had no means to pay for them, the supply of industrial goods from Europe and North America declined accordingly. Latin America was to enter a period of industrial development based upon "import-substitution", that is, making itself what it had previously imported. Peron's Argentina and Vargas' Brazil are instances of the government taking a positive role in industrialization – which example had spread to the whole of Latin America by the 1950s. Latin American governments "modernized" their countries by providing an adequate infrastructure to encourage industries as well as by nationalizing important industries, like tin in Bolivia in the 1950s and copper in Chile and oil in Venezuela in the 1970s. Governments have also developed new industries like the steelworks at Volta Redonda in Brazil and Huachipato in Chile. Even the Caribbean island of Trinidad developed its own

23

18 The Coca-Cola company is but one example of the way in which North American companies have penetrated Latin America, not always with positive results.

steel complex in the 1970s. By 1980 Brazil was producing more steel than Great Britain.

Yet it is apparent that, despite governments' greater control over the economy, for the great majority of Latin Americans there has been little or no improvement in their standard of living. The growth of industries from the 1950s to the present could be said to have made conditions worse for many people. The cost of living has been raised because home-produced goods, often subsidized, are higher-priced than their imported counterparts, kept out by government controls. Nor have the new industries always brought the hoped-for employment opportunities and they have contributed to the concentrations of misery around Latin America's cities.

Paradoxically, too, the attempt to reduce dependence on Europe and North America, through import-substitution, has largely back-fired. Capital had to be obtained in massive quantities from the world's bankers, leading to catastrophic levels of debt by the 1980s.

Technology could only be obtained by accepting the presence of multi- (or trans-)national companies on a large scale. This results in costly payments for the importation of raw materials, equipment and spare parts as well as for the rights to manufacture particular products. It also puts the Latin American host of multi-national companies in a disadvantageous situation, knowing that the multi-national company calculates its profits and losses on a global basis and could well pull out of a country if it felt that conditions were not right. The experience of Chile in the 1970s, where ITT offered the US government $1 million for the overthrow of President Salvador Allende, is but one example of the power that multi-nationals wield, or think they wield.

BRAZIL'S ECONOMIC MIRACLE

Up to the 1930s Brazil was a typical colony producing raw materials and coffee for the industrialized nations. The depression of the 1930s pushed Brazil to industrialize and to

19 Cheap labour has contributed to Brazil's "economic miracle". The other side of the miracle has been the growth of poverty and suffering.

20 There are fewer educational opportunities for women in Latin America, hence fewer job opportunities. Light assembly work of this kind, usually for multi-national companies taking advantage of cheap labour, is the highest kind of work most women can aspire to.

produce for her own market. Under President Getulio Vargas, Brazilian industry was encouraged and supported.

Kubitschek, the President after Vargas, continued with the policy of industrialization, the most notable project being the development of the Brazilian car industry. Foreign investment began to flow into Brazil and economic growth rates of 8 per cent per year – three times the Latin American average – were recorded in the period 1955-60

The military take-over in 1964 saw a further surge in industrialization, based upon the foundation laid by Vargas and Kubitschek. Strict control of society by the military facilitated a wage freeze and direction of trade unions. The state took on a central role in the running of the economy.

By the 1980s Brazil's industrialization is a reality, albeit unevenly distributed throughout the country. No other Latin American country can match the size, scope and development of industry in Brazil. By 1980 there were over 10 million Brazilian-made cars on the road, and in 1979 car production exceeded one million a year. Allied to the car industry has been the development of Brazilian steel; by the 1980s Brazil was one of the world's top ten steel producers.

Brazil possesses a range of industries making her self-sufficient in radios, TV sets and a variety of consumer goods. Brazil even has her own aircraft industry, EMBRAER, a huge merchant fleet and a thriving ship-building industry.

Brazil's "miracle" of industrialization was based primarily upon investment from abroad which by 1983 had led to debts of some US $91 thousand million. Brazil, along with other Latin American countries, was affected by the world economic crisis and found herself unable to pay the interest on her staggeringly high loans. After re-negotiating her debts to foreign banks, and so avoiding "bankruptcy", Brazil's economic problems remained and are unlikely to change until the late 1980s.

There is another side to the "miracle". The growth of Brazil's economy was accompanied by rapid urbanization and the development of extensive areas of shanty-towns around the main towns and cities. In the face of astronomic wealth made in the "miracle" by a minority, millions of Brazilians live in appalling squalor and misery. In 1984 television news around the world carried

25

pictures of starving families in the north east of Brazil, hunting through piles of rubbish, looking for food. Reports of the looting of supermarkets were common.

MEXICO'S ECONOMIC DEVELOPMENT

Mexico, like Brazil and to a lesser extent Venezuela, was well on the way to becoming an industrialized and developed country by the 1960s. The process of industrialization had been begun by President Lazaro Cardenas in the 1930s, through the nationalization of Mexico's petroleum industry, along with most of the railways. Cardenas also encouraged land reform. Later presidents were to nationalize, and so protect, the country's electric power as well as some of Mexico's developing industries. Economic growth overtook

21 Mexico's economic growth in the 1970s and '80s has been greatly aided by supplies of cheap labour. Why use machinery when there is abundant muscle-power to do the work cheaply?

population growth and Mexico appeared to be well on the road to prosperity.

The returns from Mexico's development did not affect the whole of Mexican society. Left out were the poor, rural agriculturalists who, it could be said, provided the cheap labour for Mexico's miracle. Nor was the prosperity of the 1970s, based upon the windfall of high petrol prices, wisely spent. An orgy of waste left Mexico with huge debts to repay by the 1980s.

LATIN AMERICAN INDEBTEDNESS IN THE 1980s

By 1984 Latin American countries owed the world's banks some $350 thousand million. In the 1970s the banks had been keen to lend to Latin America. The oil-producing countries of the world, following the oil price rise in 1973, were filling the

22 Protest in Mexico in 1983. The growth of trades unions, along with student organizations, has been a significant political development throughout Latin America in the twentieth century.

vaults of the world's banks with petro-dollars which the banks were looking to off-load to reliable borrowers. That is where Latin America came in.

By the end of the 1970s the bubble of prosperity had been pricked. Latin American countries found that, in the climate of a world economic crisis, the demand for their exports had fallen dramatically and, at the same time, imports of fuel, manufactured goods and capital had all risen substantially. In the autumn of 1982 Mexico almost defaulted on her huge debts, to be followed by Brazil, Argentina and Venezuela. All the Latin American countries owing money to Western banks were forced to re-schedule their debts; to ask for a longer time in which to pay off the outstanding interest on the loans. The burden was to be a huge one to bear. Most countries were put into the position of having to negotiate a loan with the International Monetary Fund (IMF), and this led to austerity measures like cuts in public spending.

In June 1984 Latin American debtors met at a "Debtors Summit" at Cartagena in Colombia. Radical proposals were made to suspend repayments, which were vetoed by Mexico and Brazil which had already entered into IMF agreements. The possibility remains of one or a number of Latin American countries opting for bankruptcy, with grave consequences for the world's banking system. Further economic development in Latin America is held back whilst the burden of debt remains. The debtor country must export, just to pay off its interest repayments; the creditor country is therefore unable to sell its own exports to Latin America. The lack of export opportunities on both sides reinforces the world economic crisis. Fidel Castro, among other Third World leaders, has advocated a moratorium on outstanding debts.

Latin American debts in 1984, in thousand millions of US dollars, stood at: Argentina 43.6; Brazil 93.0; Chile 17.9; Colombia 11.8; Mexico 89.0; Peru 11.8; Venezuela 34.0. All other Latin American countries owed considerable amounts to Western banks.

23 Vast debts threaten to mortgage the future of Latin America. The inability of Latin American countries to pay back their debts could undermine the world's banking system.

YOUNG HISTORIAN

A

1 List all the products that have historically been associated with Latin America.
2 What has held back Latin America's development? Is industrialization the answer to the pressing problems of the region?
3 Find out more about multi-national (or transnational) companies. Is their presence in a poor country beneficial?
4 How are Latin American countries to pay back the money they owe the world's banks?
5 Why did ITT want to overthrow the government of President Allende of Chile in 1973?

B

Imagine that you are a Brazilian worker in a Volkswagen factory; write about your day and that of your family.

C

Write newspaper headlines for (a) the arrival of coffee in London, (b) the discovery of *guano* in Peru (from a British and from a Peruvian viewpoint) and (c) the Latin American debt problem.

D

On a map of Latin America show the main agricultural products and industries.

REVOLUTIONS AND NON-REVOLUTIONS

Latin America has a reputation for revolutions and certainly has had its fair share. But one must distinguish between a revolution which fundamentally transforms society and *golpes*, "coups d'état" which simply usher in a new leader, even though they may be accompanied by political and social upheaval and even loss of life. Revolutions are rarely made by the most oppressed and exploited in society – if that were the case, then Latin America would be in permanent revolution – but by those whose living standards or expectations have been raised, however slightly, and who see such gains or even possible gains being taken away. Latin America has experienced both radical revolutions and *golpes*.

THE MEXICAN REVOLUTION

The origins of the Mexican Revolution are found in the instability and chaos of Mexico throughout the nineteenth century. In attempting to bring some kind of order and progress to his country in the last decades of the century, Porfirio Diaz hastened his country towards revolution. Diaz, a general in the army, seized power in 1876 and was subsequently re-elected President, sometimes by force, on seven more occasions. The *Porfiriato* (Diaz's period in power) is characterized by his attempts at economic development. Railways were built, the telegraph spread across the country, new industries were established. His *Rurales*, a tough rural police force, kept order.

The *Porfiriato* was a time of progress but the number of people affected was minute. Foreign investors were actively encouraged by Diaz's advisors, the *Cientificos*, to develop Mexico's resources. The climate provided by Diaz was excellent for foreign investors. Political dissent was ruthlessly suppressed, as were the objections of Mexican Indians whose lands were forcibly taken away from them to enlarge the *haciendas* or to provide lands for foreign investors. Diaz was oblivious to the deep-seated resentment he had caused. Most of Mexico's resources in mines, oilfields, plantations and ranches were in foreign hands, American, British, Spanish and French. The gap between the rich and the poor had increased dramatically and, not without reason, the "foreigner" was seen as responsible. Strong nationalistic feelings developed and the first stirrings of revolt were directed at Porfirio Diaz.

Francisco Madero began to oppose Diaz from 1905, declaring himself a candidate for the 1910 election. Diaz jailed Madero and subsequently exiled him to the USA. There were other stirrings of rebellion. Pancho Villa led a peasant uprising in Chihuahua; Emiliano Zapata led another in Morelos. Both uprisings demonstrated the Indian opposition to Diaz's policies of development that threatened their traditional way of life, the *ejido* system of communal landholding. The revolution's policies were taken over by the more radical demands of Zapata and, to a lesser extent, Villa, to be followed by Mexico's urban workers. Madero became President in 1911 and soon found himself under attack from Zapata, who called him a "traitor" for his moderation, and from urban

24 Pancho Villa rides with his men during the Mexican Revolution. Villa, along with Zapata, represented the Mexican country people's interests.

industrial workers. Madero was also under threat from followers of Diaz.

In February 1913, after ten days of bombing Mexico city to put down a counter-revolution, Madero was imprisoned and later murdered by General Victoriano Huerta who had been recruited by Madero to put down the rebellion threatening the revolution.

Mexico, under Huerta, entered a tragic and bloody period of civil war. Between 1910 and 1920 the population fell from 15.2 million to 14.3, as a result of the killings. Huerta was responsible for the slaying of peasant people in an attempt to get rid of the armies of Zapata and Pancho Villa. He

25 US troops in support of Carranza, in position at the Vera Cruz Customs House during the American invasion at the time of the Mexican Revolution.

had other enemies. Trying to resurrect the policies of Madero, a group known as the "constitutionalists" was set up, led by Venustiano Carranza. Supported by the US government, and in an alliance with Villa, Carranza was able to oust Huerta in 1914, although his plans were almost ruined by the over-enthusiastic support of the US government whose troops invaded the port of Vera Cruz.

The civil war continued. Carranza and Alvaro Obregon and their "constitutionalist" armies were set against Villa and Zapata. In an attempt to draw support away from the peasant leaders, Carranza granted many of the peasants' demands. In 1915 he agreed a sweeping social reform: land reform, self-government for the municipalities, labour laws and the protection of Indians' rights. But it was military victories in 1915 that finally established Carranza's power. Zapata was later treacherously assassinated in 1919; Villa killed in 1923.

Even with Carranza in command of most of Mexico, the civil war continued. In 1920 Carranza himself was murdered and Obregon became President, this signalling the end to the internal tragedy that Mexico had suffered for the previous ten years. Yet considerable benefits had been derived from the disorder and loss of life. Not least was the 1917 Constitution.

THE 1917 MEXICAN CONSTITUTION

Mexico's Constitution of 1917 was the most advanced and progressive legislation of its time. It was to be the model for other Latin American nations' constitutions in the years following.

Carranza decided in 1916 that a new constitution was necessary, to take account of the changes wrought by the revolution. The injustices done to Mexico's Indian population were righted in articles which restored ownership of the land to the nation and gave back all *ejidos*, the communal land of the Indian peasantry, that had been taken since the *Porfiriato*.

Further articles in the Constitution gave protection to industrial workers, laid down a minimum wage and an eight-hour day, arbitration for disputes, rights to belong to trade unions and

rights to strike. Child labour and *peonage*, virtual slavery, were abolished along with the *tienda de raya*, the shop owned by the *hacendado*, the big landowners, which kept the Indian peasantry in a state of *peonage*.

The Church's powers were restricted and it was forbidden to own property. Religious schools were abolished. The power of the government was also curbed by making it answerable to the Congress and the powers of the Congress were defined in economic and other matters.

THE FROZEN REVOLUTION?

Obregon lasted as President until the elections of 1924, when he was replaced by Plutarco Calles. Calles left little mark on Mexico other than to enable his Minister of Education, the writer José Vasconcelos, to establish Mexican education and

26 Diego Rivera decorated the outside of his studio in Mexico City with this mural. Others, on a much larger and more colourful scale, decorate public buildings throughout Mexico, celebrating the struggles of the Mexican people.

stimulate artistic works. The muralists of the revolution, Diego Rivera, David Siqueiros and José Orozco, trod the same ground as the Aztecs in their decoration of public buildings. The murals were an expression of the radical side of the revolution which was continued by Calles.

His continued attacks on the Church, the closing of the religious schools and the deportation of foreign priests led to the rise of the *Cristeros*, Catholic fanatics who attacked secular teachers and burned schools. The *Cristeros* were brutally put down by the government and the Church lost support.

Calles pressed on with land reform and made foreign exploiters of the oil-fields sign leases for continued use. Although he considered himself a

31

◄ 27 This statue in Cuernavaca, Mexico, was erected to commemorate the beginnings of land reform in Mexico and depicts Zapata (on the left) and Cardenas (on the right), the two architects of land reform.

socialist, Calles effectively "froze" the revolution by organizing in 1928 the PNR, the National Revolutionary Party (later called the PRI, the Institutional Revolutionary Party). By the 1930s the revolution was contained within the PRI and appeared to have run out of steam.

Lazaro Cardenas, who succeeded Calles in 1934, injected life again into the revolution by speeding up land reform, revising and encouraging trade unions and expropriating and nationalizing Mexico's oil industry. The *ejido* system of land tenure, which Zapata had advocated, became a reality for Mexico's peasantry. Cardenas's actions would, in earlier or later times, have brought down the wrath of the US, but this was the time of the "Good Neighbour Policy". The US needed the support of her neighbours especially as a second world war was in the offing.

During the war Mexico and the US became allies against the Axis in 1942. Mexico's new President, Avila Camacho, had none of Cardenas's radicalism and under him the communal *ejido* system lost the government's support. But PEMEX, Mexico's nationalized oil and natural gas industry, grew in strength and provided the foundation for Mexico's industrialization. Industry rather than *ejido* was given priority. The revolution existed only within the title of the PRI.

THE BOLIVIAN REVOLUTION

The Bolivian Revolution has much in common with its counterpart in Mexico. Both were agrarian revolutions, radicalized by the demands of their Indian peasant peoples. In Bolivia most Indians lived in the harsh conditions of the *Altiplano*, twelve thousand feet up in the Andes. Most were illiterate and played no part in society. The main resources, as in Mexico, were developed without Bolivia's interests in mind. The Bolivian Revolution was able to make fundamental changes but of a limited nature and, like the

28 The Mexican Revolution may be dead, but there is still life in the revolutionary tradition on which the Institutional Revolutionary Party (PRI) still trades. Only at election times do most Mexican people have any contact with the political life of their country.

Mexican Revolution, Bolivia's was effectively "frozen" by the 1960s.

THE WAR OF THE PACIFIC (1879-83)

The origins of Bolivia's revolution can be traced as far back as the War of the Pacific, which began in 1879. Melgarejo, President from 1865-71, treated Bolivia as his own private fiefdom. He sold Indian lands, part of Bolivia, to Brazil and gave Chile rights to mine Bolivia's valuable nitrate deposits. In an attempt to regain these deposits, upon which Chile was becoming prosperous, Bolivia claimed the nitrate mines around Antofagasto. At the same time Peru had seized nitrate works at Tarapaca. Chile declared war, relying upon her superior, British-trained navy. In 1883 a settlement was reached under which Chile was to keep the most important nitrate areas. Both Peru and Bolivia were devastated by the war, more so Bolivia which lost her outlet to the Pacific.

THE CHACO WAR (1932-35)

Having lost her outlet to the Pacific in the war with Chile at the end of the nineteenth century, Bolivia was led into a further war, against Paraguay, in a vain attempt to reach the Pacific via the Paraguay river. The possibility of there being oil deposits in the Gran Chaco region, a vast, inhospitable plain bordering Bolivia, Paraguay and Argentina, made the idea of war attractive to Bolivia. The war was a disaster for all concerned, especially Bolivia. Over 100,500 died in the war. Most were Bolivian Indians from the *Altiplano*, high in the Andes, who were out of place in the heat and lowlands of the Chaco. Paraguay was the victor in the war which did nothing to contribute to political stability in the country which suffered a string of military dictators until 1954. General Alfredo Stroessner took power in that year, maintaining himself in office thereafter through, when necessary, the most vicious forms of coercion.

Bolivia's defeat in the Chaco War led to a

29 An insurrection in 1943 in Bolivia put Major Villaroel into the presidency. His two and a half-year rule ended when he was hanged in La Paz. The unrest of the 1940s paved the way for the revolution in the 1950s.

questioning of the generation which had taken the country into the war. Nor was the Chaco War the only cause for examination. The price of tin, the main export commodity, had progressively declined on the world's markets, leading to a lowering of living standards for all, but which had especially affected Bolivia's middle class. It was the middle class, denied what they regarded as their rightful position in society, who led the pressures for reform. Affected elements within the army also sought change, as did the organized and politicized tin-mineworkers.

THE BOLIVIAN NATIONAL REVOLUTION (1952)

The formation in 1941 of the MNR, the National Revolutionary Movement, by Victor Paz-Estensorro reflected the mood for change in Bolivia. But it was not a mood shared by the whole population, not least of its opponents being the army, which kept the MNR out of office after their victories in the 1951 election. The revolution of 1952, led by the elected Vice-President Hernan Siles Suazo and Juan Lechin, a trade union leader, was necessary, even at the cost of 3,000 lives, to put the MNR and Paz-Estensorro into power. The aims of the MNR were to effect a far-reaching land reform, improve the country's communications and nationalize the tin-mines. An important part of the revolution was to bring the Bolivian Indian people more into the swing of Bolivian life and society, no easy task with a people who had maintained a life-style virtually unchanged from pre-colonial times.

Both tin production after nationalization and agriculture declined. Tin-miners, however, as well as peasant farmers, enjoyed a higher standard of living and a greater sense of well-being. The change of term from the dismissive *Indio* (Indian) to *Campesino* (country-person) was one small but significant change in society's attitude to the majority of Bolivia's population.

Paz-Estensorro was in power from 1952-56 and then from 1960-64, alternating with Siles Suazo. General René Barrientos took power in 1964, the first of a long line of military presidents, who made little impact on the basic problems of Bolivia's social and economic development.

CHE GUEVARA IN BOLIVIA

That the 1952 Revolution had made little lasting change was demonstrated in the late 1960s when Ernesto Che Guevara led a group of revolutionaries to Bolivia in the anticipation that the grinding poverty, illiteracy, lack of basic health care and other deprivations would make the country ripe for revolution.

Che was hunted down in 1967, captured and shot by Bolivian troops assisted by Brazilian and US forces. Sporadic attempts at revolution have occurred in Bolivia since then.

ARGENTINA

At the beginning of the twentieth century Argentina was enjoying an economic boom. The *pampa*, the vast fertile plain of Argentina, had been settled, and ranches and railways began the country's development. Immigrants flowed in in millions; ports and cities like Buenos Aires prospered and grew. Cereals and meat produced on the *pampas* were exported to Europe, especially to Great Britain. British capital flowed to Argentina.

There were political as well as economic changes. The vote was finally given to all adult males in 1912, after agitation from the end of the nineteenth century, and this allowed the rise of the Radical Party which had opposed the old Aristocratic politicians since its foundation in 1890. Hipolito Irigoyen, the Radical Party's leader, was elected President in 1916. Irigoyen was a disappointment to those who had elected him, who pulled his coach through the streets of Buenos Aires at his inauguration. Even though he rode to work alongside everybody else by trolley-bus, and gave his salary to charity, the hoped-for reforms did not come. Those that did had little effect, like the very limited labour reform which laid down minimum wages and maximum hours for workers. Yet Irigoyen was returned to the presidency in 1928, on account of the country's continuing prosperity based upon meat and cereal exports.

In the 1930s, however, Argentina's prosperity began to fade as the world depression made itself felt. Irigoyen was swept aside, to be replaced by a succession of presidents unable, or unwilling, to provide the type of leadership necessary for Argentina's development. In 1943 a nationalist military coup occurred that enabled the rise of Juan Peron, who was to make a lasting impression upon Argentina.

PERONISM

Juan Peron led the GOU, the Group of United Officers, in the coup of 1943. He was made Vice-President with responsibility for labour and welfare, and this enabled him to build up support through a range of reforms. He encouraged strong trade unions in the *frigorificos*, the meat-chilling plants, and made employers respond to trade union demands. Wages were increased, the eight-hour day instituted and minimum wages laid down. Peron was appealing to a new phenomenon in Argentina, a working class to whom, by his reforms, he was helping to give a sense of identity and purpose.

Fearing the growth of Peron's popularity, an army group imprisoned him in 1945, but he was freed by thousands of *Descamisados* (the shirtless), organized on the streets of Buenos Aires by trade unionists and, above all, by his wife-to-be, Eva Duarte. It was the *Descamisados* who elected him to the presidency in 1946. Peron spoke of what was occurring in Argentina as a revolution, not a political revolution, but a moral and national revolution.

Justicialism was the name Peron gave to the ideology of the Argentinian "revolution": "what we want is to do away with exploitation under whatever guise...". Nationalism was a strong part of Peron's ideology. In fact, he wanted to establish Argentina in a position between those of the US and the USSR; neither capitalist nor communist.

30 Latin American countries take a great interest in one another's political affairs. The overthrow in 1958 of Marcos Pérez Jiménez, Venezuela's dictator President, was the occasion for Argentinians and Venezuelans in Argentina to "hang" effigies of Pérez Jiménez and Trujillo of the Dominican Republic, two of Latin America's dictators.

What he developed was a form of capitalism guided strongly by the state.

The state took on the role of buying and selling Argentina's produce, and this gave it the means to buy out the English and French railways and the gas and telephone companies belonging to the US. The first Five Year Plan started in 1947 to begin public works and industrialization. Peron was convinced that only through industrialization could the standard of living of Argentinians be raised.

Peron's wife, Eva – Evita, as she was popularly known – played an important role in the "revolution". It was Evita (little Eva) who had organized the *Descamisados* to free Peron from prison and, working at his side in the *Casa Rosada*, the Pink House of the President, she organized charities on a massive scale. The Eva Peron Foundation, using state money as well as donations, established hospitals and clinics in working-class districts and generally mobilized support for Peron.

Evita came from a humble background and was a moderately talented actress and radio announcer before being propelled onto the Argentine, and international, political stage as the wife of Argentina's President. Tragically, she died of cancer in 1952, campaigning to the last to change the lot of the common people of Argentina from whose ranks she had come.

The fall of Peron came after Evita's death. The economic boom had ended, inflation affected everyone and the corruption of his administration became a scandal. Peron even broke with the Catholic Church which had supported his policies, when he separated Church from state and banned religious education in schools. With the news that his government had been excommunicated, the navy bombed the President's Palace in June 1955 but their attack did not dislodge Peron. Just two months later the army rose against him, fearing that workers might be armed to defend his regime. Peron was forced into exile for the next seventeen years but returned in 1972 to enjoy a short return to power before his death.

Peronism remained, even though the Peronist party was outlawed by the first military presidents after Peron's overthrow. Civilian government, under President Frondizi, lasted from 1958 to 1962, then again from 1963 to 1966

31 Juan Peron's return to Argentina in the early 1970s was a time to celebrate not only his, and his wife Isabel's, return but also the memory of Evita, his first wife.

when the military came out from behind the scenes to wield power personally.

The return of Peron was, even for him, remarkable. The military coup of 1966 had seen the closure of congress and the banning of all political parties. Riots and urban terrorism in 1969 and 1970 saw a new president, Lanusse, who allowed the return of political parties. Peron was allowed to return to Argentina, bringing with him the body of Evita for burial. In 1973 Peron was once again President but in name only. He was feeble and ill and died the following year. Argentina entered a further period of harsh military rule, dissolved after defeat in the Malvinas War against Britain.

Peron's contribution to Argentina was his "modernization" of the economy and society. He

◄ **32   15,000 people – men, women and even babies – "disappeared" between 1976 and 1981, during the time of harsh military rule in Argentina. This woman, along with many others, demonstrated every day in the Plaza de Mayo, Buenos Aires' most important square, for information about her missing son.**

established trade unions and protection for workers, created public services, nationalized Argentina's infrastructure and raised the standard of living as well as the consciousness of most Argentinians. Peronism continues to exist, even without Peron, claimed by both Left and Right.

THE MALVINAS WAR (1982)

In 1833 British troops invaded and occupied the Malvinas Islands in the South Atlantic, expelling their Argentinian authorities and inhabitants. Argentina continued to challenge what she regarded as Britain's illegal possession of her territories. Negotiations to resolve the dispute continued throughout the twentieth century. In the 1960s, at the request of the Security Council of the United Nations, the two countries met but were unable to agree upon a solution.

In 1981 Argentinian hopes were raised that Britain's attitude was changing. The Nationality Bill, then before the British Parliament, would take away Falkland Islanders' (the British name for the Malvinas) rights to residence in Britain and the only British naval vessel in the South Atlantic, HMS *Endurance*, was to be scrapped.

33 Argentinian soldiers waiting to go home from Port Stanley, capital of the Malvinas/Falkland Islands, at the end of fighting in 1982.

34 March 1983. The Union Jack goes up in flames outside the Bank of London and South America in Buenos Aires, in a demonstration of protest against the continuation of British control of the Malvinas Islands.

Tension rose between the two countries again in early 1982 when it was apparent that Britain had no intention of giving up the Malvinas/Falklands. In March 1982, fearing an Argentine seizure, British ships were despatched to the area. After the severing of diplomatic links between the two countries, Argentina seized the Malvinas Islands and their tiny dependencies.

Britain's response was to send a vast task force to the area. Throughout May and June Britain and Argentina were caught up in a fierce and bloody war that resulted in the loss of more than a thousand lives, most of them young Argentinian soldiers. The bloodshed ended with the Argentine surrender on 15 June 1982. Almost immediately, President Galtieri, who had taken his country to war and defeat, was ousted from government and eventually replaced by President Raul Alfonsin, who took on the difficult task of restoring Argentina to normality after the war. Alfonsin continued with Argentina's claim to the islands in the South Atlantic which were rapidly being converted into "fortresses", at huge expense, by the British government. Britain seriously damaged her relations with Latin America through her pursuit of the war and so too did the USA, because of the support she had given Britain.

BRAZIL

Brazil entered the twentieth century in a mood of relative quiet and optimism following the upheavals of the late nineteenth century. From its reputation as a "crowned democracy", the Brazilian Empire was swept away in a bloodless coup in 1889 and a republic was established. Economic and political instability characterized Brazil into the next century, and, although vast, the country was yet to be united as a nation. It was Getulio Vargas, from 1930-45 and 1950-54, who was to unify and set Brazil on the path to development.

There had been three unsuccessful revolts in the 1920s, before Vargas. None was able to attract enough support to overthrow the existing order, but all paved the way for the later transformation of Brazil. Discontents were channelled into demands for better government at state and national levels, more control over Brazilian resources and the freedoms enjoyed elsewhere in the continent. Much of the unrest of the 1920s, however, was based upon the falling fortune of coffee, Brazil's most important export, which had enjoyed high prices immediately after World War I, only to fall disastrously thereafter.

VARGAS IN POWER (1930-45; 1950-54)

Power in Brazil had been juggled between two states, Saō Paulo and Minas Gerais, which had taken turns in providing the country's President. In 1930 it was the turn of Minas Gerais, but the then President's choice of successor was from Saō Paulo. Vargas, who was governor of Rio Grande Do Sul, was put up as candidate by the Mineiros (from Minas Gerais) only to be defeated in the elections. Yet Vargas had much popular support which put him in power despite his defeat at the polls. Brazil's "revolution" had begun.

Like Peron, Vargas sought to transform his country's society and economy, the latter being as affected as any by the inter-war crisis. Welfare, medical care, housing and higher wages were provided for Brazil's working class, and ambitious plans made for Brazil's development. Industries were encouraged by keeping out foreign competition and an effective transportation system was constructed.

Vargas was popular amongst Brazil's people but was under threat from a number of quarters in his first period as President. In 1932 the *Paulistas*, from Saō Paulo, rebelled because their presidential candidate, and hence their control of Brazil's affairs, had been displaced. Then, in 1935, a Socialist/Communist alliance made an unsuccessful attempt to displace Vargas. In 1938 the *Integralistas*, a bizarre fascist group, attacked the presidential Guanabara Palace and were held off by Vargas, his daughter and a few guards until help arrived. In 1945 the army led dissatisfied groups to force Vargas to resign.

But, in 1950, Vargas had returned as President, though in a much weaker position than before.

35 **President Getulio Vargas of Brazil speaks to a Brazilian soldier en route to the war in Germany in 1942. Vargas depended upon the support of the military for both periods in power and by so doing laid the foundations for the intrusion of the military into politics after 1964.**

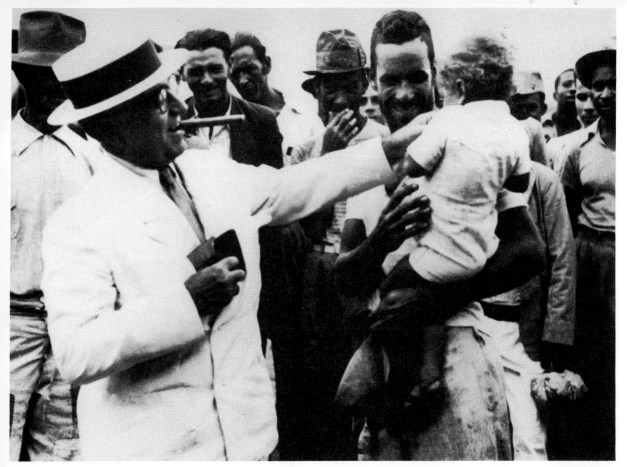

36 Vargas meets the people. In his two periods as President of Brazil, Vargas did much to unify the country, and to begin her industrialization, and made some progress in improving the worst conditions of the poor.

Nonetheless, he pressed on with plans to advance Brazil's development. He had already overseen a Five Year Plan, including an ambitious steel plant at Volta Redonda, and reformed the education system so as to cope with the demands of Brazil's development. The Second World War did much to expand Brazil's industries. Frustrated by the pressures of office, Vargas committed suicide in 1954; "I gave you my life. Now I offer you my death."

"*Getulism*", Vargas' ideology, like Peronism, is a confused ideology. Both Vargas and Peron were influenced by European fascist ideas, although neither could be labelled "fascist", despite attempts at the time to do so. When, in 1937, Vargas dissolved Congress and installed himself in power for another term and launched the *Estado Novo* (New State), many thought that fascism had arrived in the Americas. Yet the *Integralistas*, Brazil's *real* fascist party, had been banned. (Others saw communism in the *Estado Novo*.)

Rather, the *Estado Novo* gave Vargas greater power, which was generally used to the people's advantage. He used his power for the industrialization of Brazil. Unlike dictators elsewhere, he treated his enemies leniently. His successes were in uniting Brazil as a nation as never before and putting her on the road to development in a Brazilian mould. He was also responsible for giving the Brazilian military a political role which was used with unparalleled arrogance and brutality from the 1960s to the 1980s. Vargas, like Peron, is claimed by Right and Left as their own champion, indicating his essentially populist appeal.

CHILE

Chile emerged from the War of the Pacific (1879-

39

83) both prosperous and powerful, controlling the valuable nitrate resources of the region (although these were owned largely by British interests). But the stability of Chile, unique in Latin America in the nineteenth century, was destroyed in a civil war in the 1880s and '90s. The authority of the President was challenged by those who wished to replace it with control by Congress. President Balmaceda, with the Chilean army, fought against Congressional forces from the north and was defeated in two decisive battles in August 1891. Balmaceda committed suicide. Chile's Congress was to wield enormous power from that point on.

To nitrates were added copper discoveries in the first years of the twentieth century; these brought more wealth but increased economic instability. Chile depended upon the fortunes of the two commodities. The First World War generated great demand for both nitrates and copper. When the wartime boom was over, however, both industries suffered recession. Nitrates suffered more than copper, as substitutes for explosives and fertilizers had been developed out of necessity during the war. Copper became the keystone of Chile's economy (albeit in the hands of three large US companies).

Unrest following the First World War brought Arturo Alessandri to power in 1920, on the promise of a "revolution". It was not to be. Alessandri, called "the lion of Tarapaca", was thwarted at every turn by a recalcitrant Congress. He was ousted in a military coup in 1924, only to be brought back the following year. In 1927 Alessandri again was ousted in a military coup. A dictatorship followed until 1932, when he was once more elected to power to run his full term of six years. This time there was no promise of "revolution"; Alessandri was now no longer a radical.

But there were others who were. The Radical Party joined with socialists and communists to make the Popular Front Government in 1938, led by Pedro Aguirre Cerda. The Popular Front Government was to intervene in Chile's industrial development as well as to promote social and welfare legislation. One of the most important

37 Soldiers shoot down strikers in the slums of Santiago de Chile in 1962. In 1973 the army, led by General Pinochet, was to overthrow President Salvador Allende. Some historians have written of the "neutral" role of the army in Chile.

interventions was the creation of CORFO, a national development corporation that stimulated later development in industries like steel and hydro-electric power. Large farmers benefited from the corporation. The initial high expectations of CORFO have not been realized, largely because of the apathy of successive governments.

The Popular Front ceased to exist in Chile by 1941, but the radical, socialist and communist ideas remained. In 1946 Gabriel Gonzalez Videla was elected with communist support, for the promise of three Cabinet positions. With signs of the growth of communist support, Gonzalez Videla banned the Communist Party and broke relations with the USSR. From 1948-58 the Communist Party of Chile was officially banned, but economic difficulties, not least the falling price of copper and declining exports, ensured its survival.

Throughout the 1950s a succession of presidents did little to attack Chile's basic social and economic ills. By the 1960s more radical policies were favoured by Chileans. The 1958 election was a sign of things to come. A three-cornered fight saw the Conservatives, led by Jorge Alessandri (son of Arturo), triumph over the Christian Democrats and the Popular Front made up largely of socialists and communists.

The 1964 elections witnessed the triumph of the Christian Democrats, led by Eduardo Frei, whose attempts at modest reforms were blocked by opposition of Right and Left in Congress. Chile's "Revolution in Freedom", a model for Latin America different from that offered by the Cuban Revolution of 1959, failed to materialize. The 1970 election in Chile saw the Marxist Dr Salvador Allende elected President.

CHILEAN SOCIALISM

Radical and socialist ideas, as we have seen, were of long standing in Chile. Eduardo Frei's Christian Democrats offered a parliamentary, democratic form of socialism and were able to begin social and economic reform despite Congressional resistance. A land reform of 1967 saw the redistribution of some 15 million acres and the expropriation of large landholdings. The copper industry was "Chileanized", with Chile taking 51 per cent ownership in the country's largest mine. This gave no greater control of production and prices elsewhere and Chile, along with other copper producers like Peru, Zambia and the Congo, faced falling prices for her main export. It was perhaps seeking more radical solutions to their problems that Chileans voted for the Popular Unity Party (UP) of Salvador Allende.

Allende began his presidency severely handicapped, receiving only a plurality, 36.3 per cent, and not a clear majority in the 1970 elections. What distinguished Allende from previous presidents was his determination to move Chile along a socialist path to development, with a government that would be "nationalist, popular, democratic and revolutionary, that will move towards socialism".

The largest copper mines were completely nationalized, together with banks and other industries. In land reform, as many large holdings were taken over in a year and a half as in the previous six years of Frei. Unemployment was reduced, despite inflation, from 9 per cent to 3 per cent, and wages increased. Not surprisingly, most of Allende's support came from working-class and peasant people of Chile, those most benefiting from his policies. The middle and upper classes were virtually unanimous in their opposition to him, as was the United States government of Richard Nixon.

In 1974 Nixon was forced to resign as US President for illegal activities, among them responsibility for the burglary of the Watergate building in Washington to gain access to the campaign plans of his Democratic rivals. The Church Committee hearings of the US Senate in 1975, in the wake of "Watergate", showed the extent of US interference in Chile's affairs.

The Church Committee Report
Techniques of Covert Action
Expenditure in Chile, 1963-1973
  (to nearest $100,000)

Techniques:
Propaganda for Elections and other
  support for Political Parties $8,000,000
Producing and Disseminating
  Propaganda and supporting
  mass media $4,300,000

38 Any book, poster, or pamphlet which displeased the military junta ruling Chile after 1973 was publicly burned. Not so public were the tortures and killings of thousands of Chilean people by the military. (A cartoon of 1973.)

39 Augusto Pinochet, Commander-in-Chief of the Army and President of Chile after the military coup of September 1973.

Influencing Chilean Institutions: (labour, students, peasants, women) and supporting Private Sector organizations — $900,000

Promoting Military Coup d'Etat — $200,000

(Hearings before the Select Committee to Study Governmental Operations with respect to Intelligence activities. Washington, 1976)

These "accounts" were presented as an exhibit at the US Senate Hearings in December 1975. They are a damning indictment of the actions of the richest and most powerful country in the world, in exerting her will over a sovereign nation in Latin America. There is no doubt that US actions in Chile were part of the reason for the downfall of Salvador Allende, the imposition of a vicious military rule and the loss of life and erosion of human rights. Control of the Chilean economy was thereafter in the hands of economists from the University of Chicago, whose monetarist experiment in the 1970s and 1980s resulted in widespread deprivation and suffering for the mass of Chilean people.

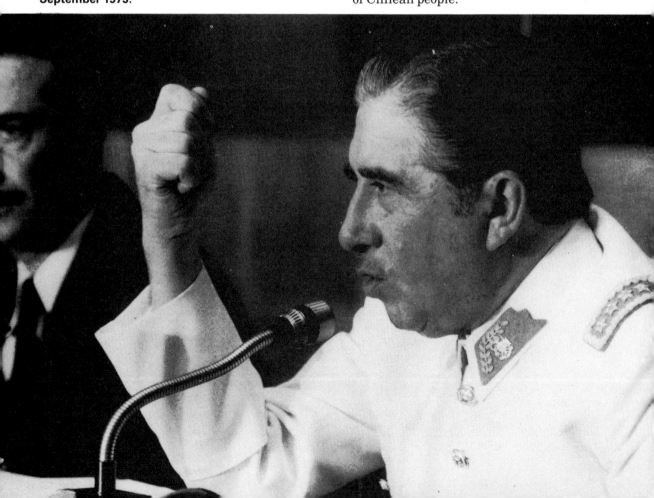

US involvement in Chile is but one example of the undercover role played by the United States in Latin America that has led to the fall of constitutionally elected presidents and to, sometimes successful, attempts on the lives of prominent politicians. The Church Committee hearings detailed numerous assassination attempts against Fidel Castro, some involving members of the Mafia. When it became publicly recognized, following the revelations of "Watergate", that the Central Intelligence Agency's (CIA) role was not just to passively collect intelligence information but to actively try to bring about the policies of the USA, even if that involved assassinations and other illegal activities, its powers were curbed, but by 1980 appeared to have been restored. A "secret war" funded by the CIA was under way in Central America to bring down the Sandinista government in Nicaragua and to ensure the defeat of struggles in El Salvador and Guatemala.

In the face of attacks from inside and outside the country, Salvador Allende pressed on with his socialist policies, only to be toppled and killed in a military-led coup in September 1973, after which General Pinochet was installed as head of a military junta.

Most of Allende's work was undone by the Junta. The mines, banks and industries were de-nationalized, the people oppressed by one of the most vicious regimes ever experienced in Latin America. Opposition was systematically eliminated. Torture and assassinations were for long the hallmark of this regime in the face of international revulsion. Thousands simply "disappeared" (as occurred under the military regime in Argentina in the 1970s).

By the 1980s opposition to Pinochet in the form of demonstrations and strikes, and of a more violent nature, began to occur in Chile. In the context of the economic collapse of Chile that was affecting all classes, Pinochet was himself under attack.

PERU

Just as it was for Bolivia, the War of the Pacific was a disaster for Peru, from which she took a long time to recover. The economy was in ruins and the country's assets were mortgaged to a British company to clear $200 million worth of debts. Presidents came and went without making much impression until Augusto B. Leguia, who ruled Peru from 1908 to 1930. He did much to stimulate the economy. Investment, mostly from the US, was encouraged and sugar and cotton were developed in the north. Towards the end of his dictatorship he improved Peru's communications, as well as public services and education. But the price was high. Leguia trampled on the constitution by having himself elected twice, and jailing and exiling his opponents.

APRA

One of those exiled was Victor Haya de la Torre who, in 1924, formed APRA, the American People's Revolutionary Alliance. Haya de la Torre combined Marxism, ideas from the Mexican Revolution and the specific conditions of Peruvian history in a powerful revolutionary ideology. APRA's appeals were for joint Latin American action against US imperialism, Latin American unity, solidarity between the oppressed and exploited, unity between intellectuals and workers, the nationalization of land and industry and internationalization of the Panama Canal.

APRA was seen as having continent-wide relevance but, although branches were founded in most Latin American countries, it only became established in Peru itself.

Haya de la Torre was never to experience power. Exiled from Peru, he could return only at Leguia's downfall to contest the 1931 election. On his defeat at the polls, supporters of APRA attempted to take power by force and several thousand of them were rounded up and shot. Haya de la Torre put his efforts into strengthening APRA. When an APRA candidate appeared to be winning the 1936 election, it was abruptly terminated and APRA was banned in Peru, on the grounds that it was an international, not a national, party.

Apristas, supporters of APRA, fought the government throughout the 1930s and until 1945, when Haya de la Torre was prepared to

DEMOCRACY

MILITARY DICTATORSHIPS

PERU

CENTURIES-OLD OPPRESSIONS

LATIN AMERICA

40 In the sixteenth century it was the Spanish "Conquistadors" who brought their own variety of oppression to Latin America; by the twentieth century it was the military who carried on the tradition. In both cases it is the humble people who have suffered most. (A cartoon of 1962.)

compromise and support the successful conservative candidate.

This was an uneasy marriage. *Apristas* sat in the Cabinet. Haya de la Torre had great authority but no power. The conservative government made no reforms. Not surprisingly, some APRA supporters rebelled, only to be crushed, an act supported by Haya himself. This was far from the end of APRA's problems. The new government was swept away in 1947 by Manuel Odria, who ruled until 1956; APRA was again banned and Haya had to spend six years in the sanctuary of the Colombian Embassy in Lima. In the 1956 elections the earlier radicalism of APRA appeared dead when Haya gave his support to the conservative candidate rather than to the radical Belaunde Terry. APRA lost more credibility in the 1962 election when Haya sided with Odria, the dictator who had caused Peru so much suffering.

Belaunde Terry was elected on his third attempt in 1963 and brought a fresh wind of change to Peru. He was a reforming President and brought land reforms, new roads, community facilities and

schools. Belaunde was overthrown in a military coup in 1968.

The next government, led by General Velasco Alvarado, was surprising in that it broke the model of previous Latin American military rule by initiating radical reforms. Lands were expropriated, Peru's oil seized and social reform begun. Peru developed good relations with Cuba where the President even underwent surgery.

By the 1980s Peru was experiencing grave economic problems because of her foreign indebtedness. Belaunde had been brought back to govern but was unable to deal with the internal needs of the country because of the huge debts. Maoist guerillas had begun to operate, with some success, in the interior.

THE CUBAN REVOLUTION

Of all the upheavals in Latin America, some of which have been revolutionary, the Cuban Revolution has been the most profound. No corner of the continent, nor of the Caribbean, has been untouched by the ripples spreading out from the stone tossed into the Caribbean pond by Fidel Castro in 1959.

Cuba, more than any of her Caribbean neighbours or any other Latin American country, had become a colony of the USA. The Spanish-Cuban-American war, that brief battle between the US and Spain, at the end of a long tradition of Cuban rebellion against Spain throughout the nineteenth century, was the realization of long-held US intentions to control Cuba.

Occupation followed invasion. US capital flowed into the island on the US's doorstep. By the 1920s the most important sections of the economy, lands, sugar, mining, were all in US hands. US ambassadors to Cuba were always the second most important political figures, sometimes *the* most important.

THE 1933 "REVOLUTION"

Fidel Castro has said that the 1959 revolution was

41 In the years immediately prior to US intervention in the Caribbean in 1898, cartoons such as this helped to mould public opinion in favour of expansion. (A cartoon of 1896.)

the result of 100 years of struggle. From the middle of the nineteenth century, Cubans fought against Spain, only to have the sought-for liberty and independence wrenched from their hands by the US invasion of 1898. The US was to play a decisive role in Cuban affairs until the revolution of 1959. The American Ambassador in Cuba also figured prominently in the abortive "revolution" of 1933.

Cuba was particularly affected by the depression of the 1930s because of her "special relationship" with the US. The political climate in Cuba was already overheated from the increasingly brutal regime of Machado. By 1933 the situation was very serious, with bloody clashes in the streets between strikers and the police.

Franklin Roosevelt, the new US President, sent Sumner Welles as his ambassador to Havana who managed to get Machado to resign. The euphoria which greeted Machado's resignation and exile was short-lived. An interim President, Cespedes, took over but failed to bring the necessary social and political reforms. Cespedes was soon in

trouble and strikes and unrest spread again through the island. "Soviets" were set up in some of the country's sugar mills, and land was seized. Strong anti-American feelings were roused by Welles's interference in Cuban politics and by the continued existence of the Platt Amendment which gave the US the right to intervene in Cuban affairs.

Cespedes was overthrown within a month of taking office, in an uprising by a group of army sergeants led by Fulgencio Batista who was then to dominate Cuban politics until the 1959 revolution. The sergeants could not govern and formed an alliance with revolutionary parties to establish a government which would be committed to economic change, a new constitution and reforms which would bring economic and social justice. Ramon Grau San Martin was made President and Batista promoted to colonel. Grau's government was split by political differences and, perhaps more ominously, the US government refused to recognize Grau's presidency. More than that, the US actively worked to get rid of Grau, through political manoeuvring, and he was forced out after barely three months as President.

Grau's departure left Batista and the US in charge of Cuban affairs, but the revolutionary feeling continued to be expressed in political and trade union unrest and this led to a general strike in March 1935. The strike was viciously put down by Batista and so this revolutionary period in Cuba's history was effectively ended, although the ideas and example were to influence the generation which made the revolution of 1959.

THE ATTACK ON THE MONCADA

The attack on the Moncada Barracks (1953) was an unsuccessful attempt to spark off a wave of revolution throughout Cuba following Batista's seizure of power in 1952. Led by Fidel Castro, the attack was designed to seize the second most important barracks in the country, from which a "Moncada Manifesto" would be broadcast, to elicit support. Cuba's second city of Santiago was chosen because of its revolutionary history extending back to the nineteenth century.

The attack was a failure. Fidel Castro was

caught, along with many other *Moncadistas*, subsequently tried and imprisoned on the Isle of Pines. At his trial, after attacking Batista for the torture and assassination of captured *Moncadistas* and announcing what measures the revolutionaries would take once in power, Castro announced: "Condemn me. It does not matter. History will absolve me."

IN THE SIERRA

Castro and the other *Moncadistas* were freed by Batista in an amnesty, after serving only eighteen months of their long sentences. Fidel Castro spent a brief period in exile, preparing for his return to Cuba to begin the armed struggle against Batista which began at the end of 1956. After an immediate, devastating setback upon landing, Castro was able to regroup a tiny remnant of his original band and begin the struggle.

Few would have thought that within two years the 26th July Movement (taking its name from the date of the attack on the Moncada) would have become a disciplined and complex organization,

42 Fidel Castro (left) with his brother Raul in their camp in the Sierra Maestra, Cuba's highest mountain range in the east of the country. Castro's guerilla army, the 26th July Movement, successfully forced Batista's troops out of this area.

that recruits and resources sufficient for the rebels' needs would have been forthcoming, and that Batista could have been politically and militarily defeated. He fled Cuba for the haven of the Dominican Republic on New Year's Eve, 1958.

THE REVOLUTION IN POWER

During the height of the "Cold War" in the early 1950s the Cuban Revolution could not have survived. It was not long before conflict developed between Cuba and the United States.

In the revolution's first years Fidel Castro was at pains to assure the world, but especially the US, that the Cuban Revolution was of a "nationalist" nature and not communist. The dramatic pace of change and the implications of the changes made convinced the US otherwise. Richard Nixon, the US Vice-President, was convinced in early 1959 that Castro was "either a communist or under communist domination". Urban and agrarian reforms, which affected US interests, drew economic as well as political responses from the US. Cuba, unable to buy essential supplies from the US, bought tractors and farm equipment from the USSR. The purchase of Soviet oil precipitated the break between the two countries and Cuba took over the running of the US and British refineries which refused to refine the oil.

Physical attacks followed the economic and verbal assaults already made and led to the US invasion of Cuba at the Bay of Pigs in 1961. On the eve of that invasion Castro announced that a socialist revolution was being made in Cuba.

SOCIALISM IN CUBA

The US-backed invasion of Cuba was quickly defeated and did much to rally support behind Fidel Castro whose government moved quickly to take a leading role in directing society and the economy. Agriculture was collectivized and the state took control of the most important industries. Education was seen as a major way of contributing to a change in consciousness and of preparing for Cuba's development. 1961 was the "Year of Education" when teachers and young men and women students went to the countryside to teach those who couldn't how to read and write. It was the start of a campaign that has lasted to the present. First, basic literacy and numeracy were the priority, then primary and secondary education. University education became a reflection of the country's economic and social needs, turning out scientists, engineers and doctors. Cuba's educational achievements would do justice to any developed country and are a shining example to the rest of the Third World.

The initial promise of elections was overtaken by the rapid changes of the first years. The revolutionary government ruled by decree. Cuba became a one-party system, in a fusion of the 26th July Movement, the Communist Party and the smaller, urban-based Revolutionary Directorate. From declaring Cuba a "socialist" state, Fidel Castro went on, later in 1961, to proclaim his own and the revolution's Marxism-Leninism.

Relations with the USSR, that had been broken by Batista, were restored in 1960. This was the first step towards the close political and economic relationship between the two countries that characterized the late 1960s, '70s and '80s. That is not to say that there were not differences. In fact, in the 1960s Cuba and the Soviet Union disagreed on more issues than they agreed upon: over Cuba's economic development, over Cuba's support for revolutionary groups in Latin America, even over Cuba's construction of socialism and communism. The 1970s were the high point of agreement and co-operation between the two countries. Cuba became a member of COMECON in 1973, closely involved with the Soviet and Eastern European economies. In the early 1980s the Soviet invasion of Afghanistan and the events in Grenada prior to the invasion in 1983, together with less favourable economic terms offered to Cuba by the USSR, had shown that important areas of disagreement still existed between the two countries, although Cuba's development was still firmly based upon her relationship with the USSR. In 1984 China and Cuba signed an economic, cultural and diplomatic agreement that heralded better relations after friction in the mid-1960s and mid-1970s.

By the 1980s Cuba's relations with the United States were, on the surface, very hostile. Fidel Castro's government had seen out the presidencies of Eisenhower, Kennedy, Johnson, Nixon, Ford and Carter. Under Reagan, relations were at their most difficult. Reagan tightened the economic blockade of Cuba that had existed from 1961 and launched a fiercely hostile diplomatic campaign against Cuba. Yet, behind the scenes, intense diplomatic activity, with secret, and not-so-secret, meetings, was taking place. Inevitably, Cuba and the USA will resolve their differences and restore diplomatic and economic relations. The timing will depend upon the terms of such an agreement and the state of world politics.

That Cuba has shown considerable development and achievement in the first twenty-five years of revolution (1959-84) is undeniable. Cuba's greatest achievements are to be found at the social level, in education, health and welfare, completely overturning the decay, corruption and lack of care that had existed under Batista. At the economic level, too, there have been advances. After the over-ambitious, and quite erroneous, experiment in rapid industrialization in the first years of the revolution and the later dislocation of the 1970 ten million tons sugar harvest, Cuba has fallen into a pattern of cautious and controlled development of agricultural diversification and industrialization. Sugar, in the 1980s, was still the most important sector of the economy and was planned to remain so until at least the year 2000, with the fluctuation of the world market still determining Cuba's economic future. A much publicized campaign to eliminate waste and increase efficiency in 1984 was an indication that long-standing problems still had to be resolved in Cuba. Having said that, Cubans were enjoying, in 1984, the best standard of living and welfare in Latin America and could expect to live to an age comparable to people in the US and Western Europe.

THE REVOLUTIONARY UPSURGE

The Cuban Revolution was the inspiration and model for revolutionary movements throughout Latin America in the 1960s. By the mid-1960s there was hardly a country in the region which did

48

The Race To The Rancho

43 The 1960s began with an upsurge of revolutionary activity throughout Latin America; the Alliance for Progress reforms were designed to combat it. By the mid-1960s the Alliance was dead. The revolutionary movements were largely contained by the end of the decade. (A cartoon of 1962.)

not have its guerilla movement forming a greater or lesser challenge to established governments.

The 26th July Movement, which had so easily defeated Batista in Cuba, was generalized into a model for revolution based upon a small nucleus of country-based revolutionaries, the *foco*. Few of the guerilla bands that followed this line of action lasted very long under combat conditions and one after another was defeated. In Argentina, Brazil, Bolivia, Colombia, the Dominican Republic, Ecuador, Paraguay and Peru the results were the same; the annihilation of the guerilla force and its leaders. That Che Guevara, Fidel Castro's close advisor, should die in the attempt to put his *foco* theories into practice in Bolivia underlined the superficial and inadequate nature of the strategy.

Che's Bolivian group and many others in Latin America were put down through the intervention of highly-trained US Special Counterinsurgency Forces. US aid and investment were the other side of the counterinsurgency coin. The rural revolutionary upsurge was contained. By the end of the 1960s another form had risen up to take its place – urban guerilla warfare. The highly-urbanized centres of Latin America, like Montevideo in Uruguay, Buenos Aires, Cordoba and Rosario in Argentina and the urban centres of Brazil, provided the "water" in which the revolutionary "fish" could swim.

In Uruguay the Tupamaros were the most prominent urban group; in Argentina the Montoneros; in Brazil a "United Front" of organizations. In all countries, despite considerable propaganda victories and notable individual successes, the urban guerillas went the same way as their rural predecessors, without achieving the overthrow of their target governments, nor the establishment of revolutionary regimes.

In the late 1970s and early 1980s, revolutionary groups were showing a greater degree of success in Central America. The Sandinistas were able to defeat and dislodge the rotten empire of the Somozas in Nicaragua; the FMLN and FDR in El

44 Geoffrey Jackson, the British Ambassador to Uruguay, was held in a "People's Prison" to draw attention to the power of the Tupamaros and to give publicity to their movement. The Tupamaros took their name from Tupac Amaru, who led Indian resistance to the Spanish in the sixteenth century.

Salvador posed a real threat to a succession of governments supported by the US, whose government poured military aid into El Salvador. In Guatemala revolutionary groups in the countryside added to the explosive nature of Central America. In Peru, a group of Maoist guerillas were established in the countryside in 1984, and in Colombia the government was forced to negotiate with the guerilla group, M19.

THE SANDINISTA REVOLUTION IN NICARAGUA

The *Sandinistas* take their name from Augusto Cesar Sandino, who led Nicaraguan resistance to US occupation in the 1920s and '30s. Like Zapata in Mexico, Sandino was assassinated and his example remained after his life.

Shortly after Sandino's death in 1934, Nicaragua began to experience the dictatorship of the Somoza family which lasted until the *Sandinistas'* victory in 1979. Within twenty years of taking power in 1936, "Tacho" Somoza was one of the richest men in Central America and by the 1970s the Somoza family owned 20,000 square kilometres of cultivable land in Nicaragua, as well as properties in Costa Rica, Mexico, the US and Canada. By the 1970s, too, the Somoza family had developed extensive business interests in banking, a variety of industries and transport services.

The dictatorship of the Somozas was dependent upon US support and their control of the National Guard. But opposition was not far from the surface. In the late 1950s a rural guerilla group inspired by Sandino began to operate in the north of the country. The success of the 26th July Movement in Cuba heartened the Sandinistas and by 1962 a group of guerilla organizations came together to form the FSLN, the Sandinista Front for National Liberation. Theirs was an uphill struggle in the face of Somoza's power and control of Nicaragua and they did, in fact, suffer many setbacks before regrouping in the mid-1970s. Somoza lost support because of the inflation that plagued the economy and the blatant way his regime pillaged the nation's resources, even profiting from the Managua earthquake. Finally, not even the US government was prepared to support Somoza and in July 1979 the Sandinistas established their revolutionary government dedicated to make Nicaragua "the second free territory of the Americas".

When the Sandinistas took over Nicaragua, the country had been ruined by civil war and they inherited a massive debt of $1,600 million. The only way forward for Nicaragua was for all sections of society to be caught up in the process of national reconstruction and development. Although committed to socialist policies, the Sandinistas persuaded businessmen and industrialists to join their cause.

As in Cuba, the Nicaraguan people were caught up in the excitement and momentum of the revolution that was being made. But just as in Cuba, the Sandinistas have evoked the wrath of the US government which has used the same kinds of economic weapons against Nicaragua as failed against Cuba. US pressures which cut off aid and investment to Nicaragua have added to existing economic and social problems. The CIA, the US government's Central Intelligence Agency, was by 1984 openly supporting counter-revolutionary groups operating against the Sandinistas from Honduras and Costa Rica. In the face of these attacks, the Sandinista government was pressing on with its economic and social programme which in the first five years of the revolution had brought work, land, education and, most of all, hope for the majority of Nicaraguans.

CENTRAL AMERICA IN CRISIS

By the late 1970s Central America, hitherto an unknown, unthought-of part of the world, often dismissed as the "Banana Republics", was figuring prominently in the world's news. The whole region seemed poised on the edge of war. In El Salvador and Guatemala the war had already broken out. In Nicaragua the Sandinista government was fighting off the "secret" and undeclared war of the United States Central Intelligence Agency (CIA) being waged from Honduras and Costa Rica.

It was in El Salvador that the war was being

fought at its fiercest and it was El Salvador which had been singled out by the US government as the country in which the line was to be drawn so as to keep out the contagious example of the Nicaraguan revolution of 1979, which had followed the Cuban example of 1959. The battle for the Western Hemisphere, according to the US government, was to be won or lost in El Salvador.

One of the smallest countries in Latin America, El Salvador's main crop is coffee, which first developed in the 1880s. 44 per cent of El Salvador's exports consist of this one crop (in 1950 it was 90 per cent), with the rest made up of manufactured goods for the North American market. Most people in El Salvador are poor; the wealth of the country is concentrated in the hands of a tiny proportion of the population. Sixty per cent of all land is owned by just 2 per cent of the people. Historically, fourteen families have controlled most of El Salvador's land and business. As in many other Latin American countries, the land is used to produce crops for export, the result being that peasant families are forced off the land and basic foodstuffs need to be imported.

The war with Honduras in 1969, the so-called "Football War", added to El Salvador's problems as refugees flooded the already congested urban areas. At about this time opposition began to show itself in El Salvador in the form of strikes and occupations. By the late 1970s El Salvador was caught up in a war being fought between government forces, supported and aided by the US government, and the Revolutionary Democratic Front (FDR), made up of all El Salvador's opposition parties and groups. Many thousands were killed and murdered in the 1980s alone, many by the security forces and right-wing paramilitary "death squads". The Archbishop of San Salvador, Archbishop Romero, was shot down by such a group whilst conducting a service in the cathedral.

Inside the United States, fearful of another Vietnam-like involvement, pressure grew to persuade the government not to increase its military commitment to El Salvador, while throughout the world demands were made for a negotiated settlement to be reached. In nearby Guatemala a similar struggle against an oligarchic government gained momentum in the 1980s. Despite US military support and aid, as in El Salvador, the guerillas were able to achieve notable successes against government forces.

YOUNG HISTORIAN

A

1 What makes a revolution? Use the example of *either* Mexico *or* Cuba *or* Bolivia *or* Nicaragua in your answer.
2 Find out more about the life of Evita Peron.
3 Write about Che Guevara in Cuba and Bolivia.
4 Find out more about fascism. Were Peron and Vargas fascist?; and if they were, did it matter?
5 Why has the United States interfered so much in Latin American politics?
6 Make a "balance sheet" of the losses and gains brought about by the Cuban Revolution.

B

Write a short biography of Fidel Castro.

C

Find out about the songs of Victor Jara who was killed in Chile in 1973.

D

Make a poster to celebrate *either* Vargas'victory in 1930, *or* Peron's return to Argentina in 1971, *or* Salvador Allende's victory in Chile in 1970, *or* the start of the Cuban Revolution in 1959.

OBSTACLES TO CHANGE

Latin America has undergone dramatic change in its history, perhaps none so dramatic as in the twentieth century. But change has varied according to country and region, and even within those countries, like Brazil and Mexico, that have shown the greatest development, an unevenness still remains. Alongside the prosperity of development, there is still deprivation and squalor; the other side of the "economic miracle".

Taken as a whole, Latin America is an underdeveloped area; illiteracy rates are high, population increases dramatically, diets are inadequate, health provision is patchy, natural resources are badly used, industrialization is uneven, agricultural productivity low, with a high degree of dependence upon foreign powers.

45   Country people in the North East of Brazil. Their crude tools alone demonstrate the need for agrarian reform.

THE LAND

One of the major obstacles to change in Latin America is the concentration of large amounts of agricultural land in a few hands. Agriculture is vitally important to Latin America, providing both raw materials and foodstuffs for domestic use and for export. For many Latin American countries agricultural products are the most important articles exported. As a result, over a third of the working population is involved in agriculture. Yet Latin America as a whole is far from self-sufficient in foodstuffs. Population growth has led to a greater demand for food, which has not been forthcoming, and many Latin American countries are now net-importers of food; whilst they may export agricultural products, like

sugar, coffee, bananas, cocoa and beef, the earnings derived from these exports are used in paying for basic foodstuffs like wheat and maize. In the period 1960-80 many Latin American countries which were previously self-sufficient in one, or more, agricultural products ceased to be so.

The increasing need to purchase food from outside the region has put a further pressure on Latin American governments already stretched for hard currency. Increased world demand for foodstuffs, which has already pushed up their prices, is likely to continue, with ominous implications for Latin America.

Landholding and cultivation in Latin America can be divided into the traditional and the modern, which often co-exist. The traditional forms date from colonial, or pre-colonial, times. Indian communal landholding, as in Mexico and the Andes, dates from before the Iberian Conquest. Also traditional, the *hacienda* system was imposed

by the Spanish and the Portuguese. Both systems imply great hardship for those who work the land. Indian land is usually held in small plots, *minifundia*, often of marginal land, as the best has gone to the large landowner, and usually cultivated for the bare subsistence of Indian families.

The *latifundia* (large landholdings) still depend upon Indian workers who are regarded as a form of cheap labour not far removed from slaves. The *hacienda* is a social and political unit, as we have seen, as well as economic. The plantations of Latin America, however efficient they may have become, also belong to the system of agriculture imposed during the colonial period.

46 Children, along with every other member of the family, must frequently work in Latin America just to stay alive. In such a situation education is not high on the list of priorities of a poor family.

The difference between those working small plots and those owning huge estates could not be more marked. Indians in Mexico, Peru or Bolivia working traditional small plots fight to stay alive. Every scrap of land is cultivated on their plots, yet even this is not sufficient. Part-time jobs have to be taken, some akin to acting as beasts of burden, in order to earn extra. Seasonal work on the *hacienda* provides a meagre supplement. Those born into subsistence farming hardly ever leave it. In those areas there is no social or medical provision, no schools that would allow the young to leave the hardships and miseries behind them. Such conditions have led to unrest in countries like Brazil, Mexico, Colombia and Peru. But, effectively, the unequal division of land has resulted in nations within nations; poor, uneducated Indian agriculturalists who have no role in the political and social life of the country.

In the large *haciendas*, life could not be more different. In contrast to the smallholder, with his inadequate and insanitary dwelling, the *hacendado* enjoys a luxurious living, treating his poorly-paid workers like children, giving handouts and support in occasional times of need. The *hacendado's* income will be hundreds of times that of his workers; yet the system is an uneconomic one. Yields are traditionally low because the *hacendado* is more interested in privilege, status and power than in maximizing his return from the land. Providing he receives a reasonable income, the *hacendado* is satisfied.

Land reform has been slow in coming to Latin America. The exception is Mexico where, as we have seen, the revolution brought about reforms in land tenure from 1915 onwards. In South America there was no land reform until the 1950s, though by the 1960s most countries had experienced some changes in landholding and use, albeit of a minor nature. Bolivia's revolution in the 1950s brought about fundamental change; in Peru the military government from 1968 also instituted radical changes. During Bolivia's revolution many large estates were seized by the landless farm labourers who worked them. The Land Reform of 1953 legalized these seizures and divided all the large estates between those who worked the land. Dividing up the land in this way is only part of the answer, for, as in the Bolivian example, land reform actually led to a fall in agricultural production (although it did subsequently rise). Land reform needs to be accompanied by financial and technical help. Credit needs to be provided for those working the land, as well as assistance with machinery and irrigation to enable the most to be derived from the soil. The lack of provision of these elements has frequently doomed land reform to failure.

THE CHURCH

The *hacienda* is one institution which has helped to maintain a *status quo* in Latin America. The Church is another. From the very moment of conquest the Church played an important role in the New World. The number of churches, cathedrals and monasteries throughout Latin America today is a physical expression of the power of the Roman Catholic Church. Nor was the Church's role purely religious. The first schools, hospitals and clinics were established by the Church, and many of them still operate in the 1980s. Even in revolutionary Cuba the Roman Catholic Church maintains a healing and caring role.

Despite curbs on the Church's powers – Mexico is one example – Roman Catholicism was usually to be found supporting whatever regime happened to be in power, however brutal and reactionary. In

47 In revolutionary Cuba there is still a role for religion. Nuns administer old people's homes and hospitals that are funded by the state which also renovates churches.

the 1960s the Church emerged from centuries of accepting, as well as reinforcing, the ills of Latin American society, to re-examine its social, economic, even political attitudes. The "Theology of Liberation" resulted. Many Church-men and Church-women repudiated the established role of the Church, which was to concentrate on salvation, and preferred instead to work with and for the poor and to press for radical solutions to the social and economic problems of the region.

In Brazil, Archbishop Dom Helder Camara, just one of the country's priests appalled at the persistence of illiteracy, poverty and misery, entered the political arena as a fierce opponent of the military government after 1964. Dom Helder was sympathetic to those who held that the only way to change society in Latin America was by taking up arms. There were other priests who actively advocated revolutions. The most prominent was the Colombian priest, Camilo Torres.

Camilo Torres found the Church's wealth in Colombia at odds with the misery of life for most Colombian people. He felt unable to serve two masters, God and mammon, and even advocated expropriating the Church. Forced to leave the Church, he devoted his energies to political work and finally joined the guerilla forces of the National Liberation Army. He was killed in an action against a government patrol. Like Che Guevara, who was killed in action the following year in Bolivia, Camilo Torres became a potent example for others to follow.

The Conference of Latin American Bishops at Medellin, Colombia in 1968 was a further element in the change running through the Church that accepted revolutionary solutions in certain circumstances: "Revolutionary insurrection may

48 Daniel Ortega, member of the Sandinista government of Nicaragua, attacks US policies in Latin America during Pope John Paul's visit to Central America in 1983. The Pope had strong words during his visit for Nicaraguan priests who are also members of the government.

49 The 1950s were seen, briefly, as a time when civilian governments had triumphed over the military variety. It was a view, and a reality, not held for long. (A cartoon of 1956.)

be legitimate in the case of evident and prolonged tyranny which dangerously threatens the common good of a country," the Conference declared. The effects of the Medellin Conference were felt throughout Latin America. In Nicaragua it resulted in priests and even the hierarchy of the Church speaking out against the excesses of the Somoza family. Members of the Church became involved with the FSLN, the Sandinista National Liberation Front, and after the overthrow of Somoza in 1979 priests accepted government positions in the face of Vatican disapproval. In

1984 the Catholic priests in cabinet positions were being pressured by the Pope to choose between their secular work and the Church.

THE MILITARY

The struggles for independence gave birth to a strong military tradition in Latin America. The military has traditionally taken a political role and few nations have been free of military intervention. In the 1960s constitutionally elected regimes in Guatemala, Ecuador, the Dominican Republic, Argentina, Peru, Bolivia and Brazil were all toppled by the military. In the 1970s Chile joined their ranks and there were further military *golpes* amongst those countries already ruled by the military.

Military intervention in Latin American politics is a paradox. On the one hand, the military sees itself, and is frequently seen, as the upholder of law, order and security. It has frequently acted on "anti-communist" crusades. Yet, at the same time, the military has been responsible for crushing constitutional and democratic

50 Isabel Peron, "Isabelita", Argentina's President from 1974-76, took power on the death of her husband Juan Peron. Isabel was overthrown in a military coup in March 1976.

institutions. For example, in Brazil in 1964 João Goulart was ousted by the military because of his "leftist" leanings, as were Frondizi in Argentina and Salvador Allende in Chile, after which each country was ruled by a vicious military regime.

The military is strong in contemporary Latin America because it represents a privileged group in society. It is well-funded by governments, receiving on average some 20-25 per cent of the budget. Some military budgets are as high as 50 per cent of a nation's budget. Most Latin American militaries are linked to the United States through military aid or training, or a shared belief in the need for security and order in the hemisphere.

Yet the familiar picture of the Latin American military acting against change and development has been modified since the 1960s. Military regimes in Peru, Panama and Bolivia, the latter very briefly, brought to their countries radical reforms that took them further along the road of development and democracy. In Cuba since the revolution, the military has performed civilian as well as military tasks, with members of the high command moving from the military to the government and back again.

The 1980s saw the discrediting of the military regime in Argentina from its defeat in the war against Britain over the Malvinas/Falkland islands. Brazil took the first steps towards democracy after twenty years of military rule, moving towards civilian government in 1985.

51 A Mexican poster. "It is not especially difficult to teach a child or adult to read and write, if this is done with enthusiasm and the spirit of patriotism." Mexico is one of the few Latin American countries to have made education a priority.

EDUCATION

The quality of life in any nation today is

fundamentally related to the level of its science and the vitality of its culture. Both, in turn, are crucially dependent on education . . . .
This lack [of highly trained people] has been especially severe in the less industrialised countries of the western hemisphere. (From the official report of a United States Presidential Mission for the Western Hemisphere, 1969)

The Mission went on to recommend the establishment of a new institution for education, science and culture, with an annual budget, *to start with*, of $100 million. It would begin to deal with the problems of illiteracy and the lack of educational facilities at all levels and to gear education to the developmental needs of the region. The Mission was fearful of the changing roles of the Church and the military, and of the growing dissatisfaction within the region based upon the misery and deprivation of the majority of people's lives.

The recommendations of the Mission were ignored and the problems in education still remained in the 1980s. Illiteracy rates were high, school provision was inadequate and higher education was rarely based upon the social and economic needs of each country. Only in those countries that had undergone profound social transformation – Cuba and Nicaragua – had education been made a priority for social and economic development.

52 Working in the home, looking after a family, selling flowers at market; this Mexican woman's day is a long, unfair and exhausting one.

SLAVES OF SLAVES: WOMEN IN LATIN AMERICA

To understand the position of women in Latin America, one must understand the term *machismo*. *Machismo* is a Spanish word and is usually associated with Latin America but it describes, of course, a world-wide phenomenon. *Machismo* is men's power over women, at work, at home and in the street. Men are seen as being superior to and more important than women. The man must come first, at mealtimes and whenever men and women are together.

But speaking to Latin American women, few would be aware of their exploitation and domination by men. To most men and women it

seems "natural" or "logical" that men and women have different roles in society, even though the women have to take a back seat. These ideas have developed over the centuries of colonialism and have taken the place of the important position of women in pre-colonial times.

In many parts of rural Latin America, both men and women suffer a miserable existence, although the misery is not always equally shared. Men and women work together in the fields, sometimes acting as beasts of burden, toiling to eke out a bare subsistence. Women must, at the same time, bear

58

and bring up children, cook and care for the family. Women, in practice, have few rights.

But it is difficult to see how Latin American women can be caught up in a process of change and transformation unless other changes occur, not least, dramatic improvements in health, education and human rights. Issues that have concerned feminists in Europe and North America, like wages for housework or equal pay for equal work, have simply no validity in a context where, say, both men *and* women receive no direct pay for the work they do in the fields. For the lot of women to improve throughout Latin America it is necessary to alter many of the other existing relationships and institutions.

YOUNG HISTORIAN

A

1 Find out more about "Liberation Theology". Why has it caused division within the Church?
2 Why is land reform so important in Latin America? Can it be brought about other than by revolution?
3 Why has education not been a priority in many Latin American countries? What has been the experience of those countries in which it has been?
4 What is *machismo*? Have you ever experienced anything like it?
5 What is meant by "underdevelopment" and "development"? Whom is "development" for?

B

Write about Dom Helder Camara of Brazil.

C

Imagine you are a woman in Latin America; write an account of your daily life.

D

On a map of Latin America show those countries where the army plays a significant political role.

THE US FACTOR

World War One was a turning point for Latin America's relations with the rest of the world and heralded the growth of US influence in the region. Before the war Great Britain had dominated trade and investment. After the war the United States had taken over, increasing her already significant economic interest. The United States' and Latin America's futures were to be intertwined.

THE MONROE DOCTRINE (1823)

The Monroe Doctrine was America's claim to Latin America following the wars of independence. In the face of a possible attempt by the Holy Alliance, a group of European powers, to "re-capture" Latin America, and fearful of the growing influence of Great Britain, the United States President, Monroe, announced that any attempt to extend the system of European monarchies to the Western hemisphere would be interpreted as "dangerous to *our* peace and safety". Further, any attempts to recapture lost colonies would be regarded as "the manifestation of an unfriendly disposition to the United States".

The United States was in no position to enforce the Monroe Doctrine until the end of the nineteenth century, as events were to show. When the French attacked Argentina in 1838 and when the French and British blockaded Buenos Aires in 1848, no amount of invoking the Doctrine had any effect. Nor did it when the French attacked Mexico in 1838 or during the French, British and Spanish attack on Vera Cruz in 1862. The British took the

Malvinas Islands from Argentina in 1833 and the north coast of Honduras two years later, ignoring the Monroe Doctrine. By the end of the nineteenth century, however, when Great Britain and Venezuela were at one another's throats over the border dispute with British Guiana, it was the

53 By the start of the twentieth century the United States was the unquestionable imperial power in Latin America. (A cartoon of 1902.)

nvoking of the Monroe Doctrine which persuaded the British to finally accept US arbitration. The US Secretary of State, Richard Olney, pointed out to Britain that: "Today the United States is practically sovereign on this continent and its fiat is law upon the subjects to which it confines its imposition."

Throughout the nineteenth century the United States had invaded Mexico, taking the richest half of her territory. In the twenty years from 1840 American "filibusters", buccaneers, were to attempt to invade parts of Latin America with their private armies. It was a sign of what was to come.

From 1898 the United States was politically, economically and militarily developed to embark upon a policy of expansion. Puerto Rico was annexed and Cuba established as a republic whose President was chosen by the US and whose constitution was written by them. The Platt Amendment (1901) gave the US the right to intervene in matters of "life, property, individual liberty" and "Cuban Independence". US forces were to intervene directly, and indirectly, in Cuba until the 1930s when the Platt Amendment was abrogated.

President Theodore Roosevelt was to add to the Monroe Doctrine. His "corollary" (1904) gave the US the "duty" to intervene to guard American investments in the Caribbean and Latin America. She was to do so some sixty times between 1900 and 1933. The Dominican Republic felt the extent of US police powers in Latin America from 1914-24. In 1912 US Marines put down a rebellion in Nicaragua, staying for the next twenty years. Haiti's occupation lasted from 1915 to 1934.

US actions, which came to be known as "Dollar Diplomacy", did much to develop anti-"Yankee" sentiments in the hemisphere. The liberator of Latin America, Simon Bolivar, had already pointed out in 1829 that, "The United States appears to be determined by Providence to plague America with misery in the name of liberty." Such sentiments were repeated by José Martí, Cuba's apostle of revolution, at the end of the nineteenth century. Martí had "lived inside the belly of the monster and knew its entrails". His fears of a US take-over from Spain at the successful conclusion of the Cuban liberation struggle were well-founded. Anti-American feeling is strong within Latin America, as US Vice-President Nixon found during his tour in Latin America in 1958. At the same time there is great admiration for the material successes of the United States.

THE US AND THE PANAMA CANAL

The idea of a canal across Central America, linking the Atlantic and Pacific oceans had occurred to the Spanish, but it was the United States, under President "Teddy" Roosevelt, who brought the idea to reality. Already a US company operated a railway across Panama, which was then part of Colombia. But it was the Spanish-American war which convinced Roosevelt of the need to be able to move troops quickly from one ocean to the other. The growth of US investment and trade with Latin America in essential raw materials was a further pressing reason for having the canal.

In January 1903 the US government negotiated with the Colombian government to build a canal across the isthmus of Panama. The Hay-Herran treaty would have given the US a 100-year lease of a 100-mile strip across the Panama isthmus for $10 million and a $25,000 annual rent. Colombia wanted more money but Roosevelt wanted his canal.

A revolution started in Panama city for the independence of Panama from Colombia, the revolutionaries receiving support from the US. The USS *Nashville* appeared on the Atlantic coast to keep out Colombian troops. Given American support for Panama, which was recognized by the US after three days of revolution, Colombia could only withdraw. President Roosevelt was to claim that US actions "had been carried out with the highest, finest and the nicest standards of public and government ethics".

The canal was built by US engineers and the Panama Canal zone came into existence administered by the United States and opened for traffic in 1914, revolutionizing the flow of goods through the region. The canal zone was ceded to the US in perpetuity, but by the 1960s Panamanians began to demand a renegotiation of their treaty with the US. This was resolved in 1979

54 Workers from all over Central America and the Caribbean contributed to the building of the Panama Canal.

when a compromise was reached which gave the canal zone back to Panama but maintained US control of the area.

Panama's action in demanding a re-evaluation of her relationship with the US was a part of the growing mood of nationalism in Latin America and its determination to limit the influences of other countries in its affairs.

THE GOOD NEIGHBOUR POLICY

America's actions in the Spanish-American War and again in enforcing her will over the Panama Canal were viewed with suspicion and concern by Latin American people. Subsequent military and

times the US would have responded unfavourably to such action. But in the context of FDR's Good Neighbour Policy there was no invasion, no economic nor diplomatic pressure. The US and British companies were compensated and Mexico/US relations entered a period of respect and co-operation. Roosevelt had to accept Cardenas' determination to develop Mexico's own resources not only for the sake of his new initiative in hemispheric policy but because World War II was on the horizon. Mexico was to enter the war in 1942.

55 Although heralded as new, the "Good Neighbour Policy" is now seen as the same policy as before but in a gentler form. The United States remained as Latin America's "policeman". (A cartoon of 1934.)

political interventions in Latin America and the Caribbean did little to erase this concern.

In his inauguration speech in March 1933 President Franklin Roosevelt announced a new era of inter-American relations based upon mutual respect and non-intervention. This was the "Good Neighbour Policy". Special trade agreements and the lowering of US tariffs were also promised. One could interpret this new policy, based upon the acceptance that in the past the US had *not* been a good neighbour, as an example of US enlightenment. Certainly, the calibre of US diplomats in Latin America was raised. But it could also be said that, in the conditions of the world depression, it was no longer practical for the US to maintain its "Big Stick" policies towards its weaker neighbours. A more conciliatory, but nonetheless effective, policy of maintaining US control of Latin America was necessary.

Mexico, in the 1930s, was led by President Cardenas, who took back the foreign-owned railways as well as the oil industry owned by US and British companies. At earlier, or even later,

"THE SARDINE AND THE SHARK": FEAR OF COMMUNISM, AND THE INVASION OF GUATEMALA (1954)

"Perhaps the mistake of the American Government had been to place too great an emphasis upon the disruptive power of communism in the Western Hemisphere, without devoting more wisdom to the analysis of the social illness which makes communism," wrote a leading American historian, Hubert Herring (*A History of Latin America*, New York, 1955).

By the 1950s fear of communism was at its highest in the US government and "cold war" was being fought between the USA and the USSR. Inevitably, Latin America was to be affected. In Guatemala the US Central Intelligence Agency (CIA) was directly involved in the overthrow of Jacobo Arbenz in 1954. Arbenz was far from being a communist, but it was enough to be a nationalist to incur the fears and wrath of the US.

Elected in 1950, Arbenz had sought to continue the reformist policies of his predecessor, Arevalo, based upon land reform and the construction of a welfare state. American interests, not least the United Fruit Company, felt threatened by the land reforms, and the anti-communist hysteria of the time was sufficient for the CIA to support the invasion into Guatemala of Carlos Castillo Armas. He was established as President and Arbenz's policies were reversed in favour of American interests.

Castillo Armas was assassinated three years after the invasion, to be replaced by a right-wing dictatorship. By the 1980s Guatemala was experiencing a civil war. Government troops, supported by the United States, by the fiercest repression sought to put down resistance to the government, which had made no progress in dealing with the social and economic backwardness of the country.

THE ALLIANCE FOR PROGRESS

The Alliance for Progress was President John Kennedy's reaction to the example of the Cuban Revolution. Its premises were sound – to bring the basic necessities of life to the people of Latin America – but it failed to live up to its promise and may even have reinforced the very ills it was set up to remedy.

56 The Cuban Revolution, usually personalized in Fidel Castro, has been seen as the source of all ills in Latin America since 1959. As this cartoon shows, Castro did not produce the social and economic injustices which are the real sources of discontent and potential revolution. (A cartoon of 1962.)

The Alliance was born at the Punta del Este conference of the Organization of American States (OAS) in Uruguay in 1961. In a message to the conference President Kennedy said the Alliance meant "full recognition for the right of all people to share fully in our progress. For there is no place in democratic life for institutions which benefit the few while denying the needs of many." The needs of the many were great and the Alliance set about meeting them, with a plan to raise per-capita incomes, eliminate illiteracy, increase low-cost housing, stabilize prices, purify water supplies, control disease and raise life expectancy among all the peoples. The Alliance also sought an increase in common markets in Latin America and a speed-up of land reform and agricultural diversification.

Even at Punta del Este there was scepticism; Cuba's representative Che Guevara was openly doubting. Reservation about the Alliance grew. This is how it was described by the Brazilian economist Josué de Castro:

> The injection of dollars does not help the people but governments whose interests are often opposed to the people's . . . .
> The Kennedy Plan, unfortunately, has been conceived more as a political plan than as an economic plan, and suffers from all the prejudices with which United States interests confuse foreign policy . . . . All of this is nothing but pure colonialism . . . . colonialism is the only cause of hunger in Latin America. (from *Mundo Economica*, Caracas, quoted in *The Great Fear in Latin America*, John Gerassi, 1968).

The plan was for $100 thousand million-worth of investment to flow to Latin America, most of it from the US, over ten years. That some schools, houses and clinics were built with Alliance money there can be no doubt, but most of it flowed to the already wealthy and not to those with no roof, no schools, no work and no land. Inflation resulted from the flow of funds, making the poor even poorer. The gap between rich and poor widened, thanks to the Alliance, rather than narrowing. Aid flowed to the most repressive regimes in Latin America, Ydigoras of Guatemala, Duvalier in Haiti, the Somoza family in Nicaragua, Stroessner of Paraguay, so reinforcing the very conditions that needed changing. By 1964 the Alliance had begun to founder, with the recognition of the military regime in Brazil and then the US invasion of the Dominican Republic the following year. So much for democracy. The Alliance for Progress began just after the US government-backed invasion of Cuba at the Bay of Pigs. In 1965 the US invaded the Dominican Republic to oust President Juan Bosch because of his left-leanings. The tiny Caribbean island of Grenada was invaded by a massive force of US marines in 1983. From 1979 the Sandinista government of Nicaragua faced a barrage of economic and diplomatic attacks whilst the Nicaraguan borders were constantly under threat from US-financed *contras* (counter-revolutionaries). The British government was one of many to object to the mining of Nicaragua's ports in the US's "secret" war on Nicaragua. A new approach to Latin America had been promised by each new US President since Franklin Roosevelt. Yet outright invasions such as these were the exception rather than the rule. The close identity of interests existing between the United States and Latin American states was such as to make such shows of force unnecessary.

YOUNG HISTORIAN

A

1 What is "imperialism"? Was US imperialism at the end of the nineteenth century the same as British imperialism in India?
2 Find out more about the "Cold War"; what did it have to do with Latin America?
3 Why did President John Kennedy allow the Bay of Pigs invasion to continue; why did it fail; and what was the long-term result?
4 Has America's policy towards Latin America changed in the twentieth century?
5 Why did the Alliance for Progress fail?

B

As a journalist you may ask any of the following US Presidents' views on Latin America: Pres. Franklin D. Roosevelt, Pres. John Kennedy, Pres. Ronald Reagan. What ten questions would you ask?

C

Write newspaper headlines for (a) the opening of the Panama Canal, (b) Teddy Roosevelt's campaign in Cuba in 1898, (c) the announcement of "the Good Neighbour Policy" in 1933 and (d) the announcement of the Alliance for Progress.

D

Show on a map of Latin America all interventions by the US from the nineteenth century to the recent past.

LATIN AMERICA IN THE WORLD

As the twentieth century comes to a close, there is little room for optimism in Latin America. For the great bulk of the population there is little to look forward to other than a continuation of the hardship and misery that have marked their lives so far. The hoped-for social and economic development of the region has not materialized and, where it has, it has not altered the lives of the majority for the better.

The debt that affects virtually every country in the region but especially Brazil, Argentina and Mexico will hold back further the possibilities for progress until the late 1980s and maybe beyond. Latin American countries, long-used to being caught up in the booms and slumps of being tied to few products and few markets, have learned another harsh lesson of their inferior position to the developed world. Yet their very indebtedness could be a weapon to be used against the European and North American creditor nations, to bring about a new economic order. Already, Latin American nations are approaching their shared problem of indebtedness jointly rather than as individuals.

Such a demonstration of co-operation and unity has favourable implications for the future if it can continue and extend the already existing channels for unity in Latin America. The Central American Common Market has shown itself to be of enormous benefit to its member countries, by cutting out imports and stimulating trade between its members, although the predominance of US investment and control remains a problem. The establishment of the Latin American Free Trade Association (LAFTA) and the Latin American Economic System (SELA) is a further positive development. All such forms of co-operation can only increase Latin American countries' bargaining power. Past attempts at Latin American co-operation in the marketing of raw materials and agricultural products have been beset by both political and organizational difficulties.

The US government's support of Britain in her war with Argentina over the Malvinas/Falkland Islands in 1982 and the US invasion of Grenada in 1983 have prompted Latin American nations to take stock of their position with the United States. What are the implications for Latin America if the US can support Britain against Argentina when she has a defense agreement with the latter, and if she can invade the tiny country of Grenada so far from the US and clearly of marginal importance in the region? There was further concern, expressed forcefully by Mexico and Venezuela, over the growing military involvement of the United States in Central America. US military aid has increased to both El Salvador and Guatemala and the "secret" offensive against Nicaragua has intensified. Under President Reagan, American economic and diplomatic pressure has also been tightened against Cuba. The fears of Bolivar and Martí about US intervention in Latin America continue to be justified.

57 Burdened by enormous debts in the 1980s, Latin American countries can only continue to trade with the rest of the world if there is a willingness to buy Latin American products in return.

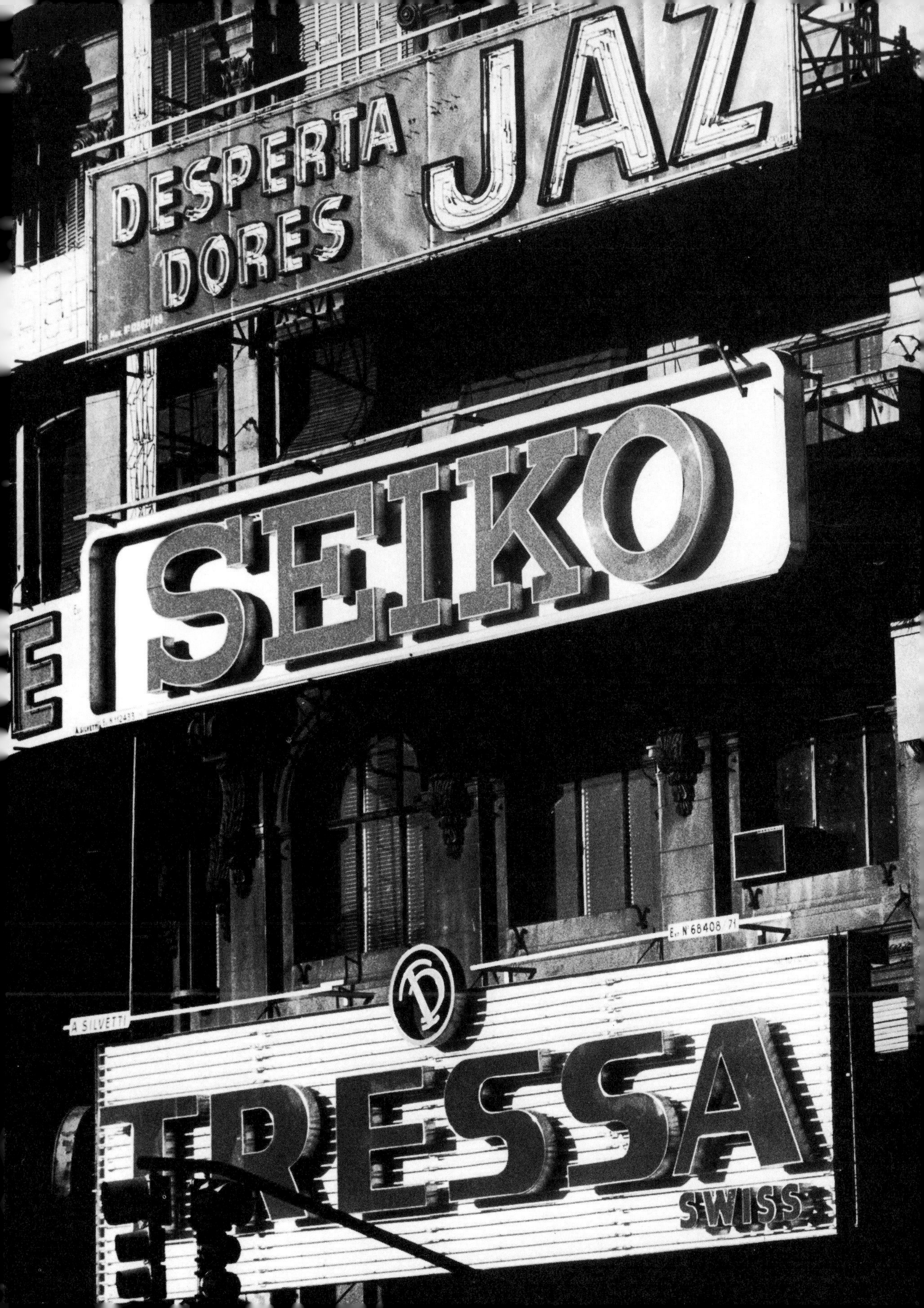
DESPERTA
DORES
JAZ
SEIKO
A SILVETTI
TRESSA
SWISS

Yet it is difficult for Latin America to break away from its dependency on the United States, cemented, as it is, by history and indebtedness. The so-called Organization of American States (OAS), formed in 1948, has largely been a reflection of US policies towards the area. Britain's prestige in the area diminished as a result of the war with Argentina and Britain could never replace the economic links of the US. Nor is it desirable that she should. For Latin American countries their best hope for the future is through the diversification of their trading relations as

58 The priorities of Brazil: *favelas* — shanty-town houses — in Brasilia, where homes are made mainly of sacking, next to newly-built government offices.

The problem for Latin America, as it is for the other countries of the Third World, is that, as a result of historical links with more powerful countries, its attempts at development have, at best, been thwarted. Only by breaking out of its dependence can Latin America realize its vast potential.

59 The stereotype image of the "Lazy Latin American" who, through his lack of commitment to reform, is about to be engulfed in a wave of revolution. Is this the reality of Latin America in the twentieth century? (An American cartoon of 1962.)

well as a diversification of their products. Industrialization is not the "magic wand" to their problems for, where domestic markets are small and where the population is badly paid when receiving payment at all, a policy of industrialization has shown itself not to work. Latin American trade with countries such as Japan and with the Middle East represents a new and positive development.

The future for Latin America can only be positive if all its people are caught up in the process of development, so releasing the wealth of human potential which at present is denied such an opportunity. Latin America has enormous natural resources which so far have been utilized for the growth and development of other countries.

YOUNG HISTORIAN

A

1 Why was the Malvinas/Falklands War fought? Write from *either* an Argentinian *or* a British position.
2 Why has the US reacted so strongly to events in Central America?
3 Can Latin America progress entirely under its own efforts?
4 Find out more about Latin American trade with countries other than the US and Europe.

B

You live in a Latin American city; write a letter home to your family in the country, telling them what is so different about your life there.

C

Make a "balance sheet" showing the strengths and weaknesses of any two Latin American countries.

D

Make a poster for the 500th anniversary of the "discovery" of the New World, in 1992.

BOOK LIST

Alonso Aguilar, "Pan Americanism from Monroe to the Present" (*Monthly Review*)

Harold Blakemore, *Latin America: Essays in Continuity and Change* (BBC)

Richard Bourne, *Political Leaders in Latin America* (Penguin)

Rosemary Bromley and Ray Bromley, *South American Development* (Cambridge University Press)

George Camacho, *Latin America: A Short History* (Allen Lane)

Bruce Chatwin, *In Patagonia* (Cape)

Simon Collier, *From Cortes to Castro* (Secker & Warburg)

Jean Franco, *The Modern Culture of Latin America* (Penguin)

Andre Gunder Frank, *Capitalism and Underdevelopment in Latin America* (Penguin)

Celso Furtado, *Economic Development in Latin America* (Cambridge University Press)

John Gerassi, *The Great Fear in Latin America* (Collier Macmillan)

Alan Gilbert, *Latin American Development* (Penguin)

John Griffiths, *The Caribbean in the Twentieth Century* (Batsford)

Irving Louis Horowitz/Josué de Castro/John Gerassi (Eds.), *Radicalism in Latin America* (Vintage)

Peter d'Λ Jones, *Since Columbus* (Heinemann)

Latin American and Caribbean Women's Collective, *Slaves of Slaves: The Challenge of Women in Latin America* (Zed)

Oscar Lewis, *Children of Sanchez* (Penguin)

Marcel Niedergang, *20 Latin Americas* (Penguin)

Jenny Pearce, *Under the Eagle: US Intervention in Central America and the Caribbean* (Latin American Books)

George Pendle, *A History of Latin America* (Penguin)

Rodolfo Stavenhagen (Ed.), *Agrarian Reform and Peasant Movements in Latin America* (Anchor)

INDEX

The numbers in **bold type** refer to figure numbers of the illustrations